I WAS A STRANGER

I Was a Stranger

Stranger

A Christian Theology of Hospitality

Arthur Sutherland

Abingdon Press
Nashville

I WAS A STRANGER
A CHRISTIAN THEOLOGY OF HOSPITALITY

Copyright © 2006 by Arthur M. Sutherland

This book is printed on acid-free paper.

Library of Congress Cataloging-in-Publication Data

Sutherland, Arthur, 1956-
  I was a stranger : a Christian theology of hospitality / Arthur Sutherland.
    p. cm.
  Includes bibliographical references.
  ISBN 0-687-06324-8 (binding: pbk., lay flat : alk. paper)
  1. Hospitality—Religious aspects—Christianity. I. Title.

BV4647 .H67 S88 2006
241'.671—dc22

2006016388

06 07 08 09 10 11 12 13 14 15—10 9 8 7 6 5 4 3 2 1

MANUFACTURED IN THE UNITED STATES OF AMERICA

Contents

Acknowledgments

I wish to thank the people, groups, and institutions that supported my effort to write this book. Grants from the Coolidge Fellowship, the Center for the Humanities at Loyola College in Maryland, and the Wabash Center for Teaching and Learning in Theology and Religion all played significant roles. Listeners at the American Academy of Religion, the Notre Dame Center for Ethics and Culture, the D. B. Reinhart Institute for Ethics in Leadership at Viterbo University in La Crosse, Wisconsin, and inmates at the Maryland State Correctional Facility in Jessup offered me the opportunity to be both applauded and criticized. The librarians at Loyola College in Maryland and Pitts Theology Library at Emory University were very helpful to me. N. Lynne Westfield, Amy Oden, and Christine Pohl, all of whom have significant works on hospitality, encouraged my work. I need to thank Sharon Watson Fluker at The Fund for Theological Education for introducing me to my editor at Abingdon Press, John Kutsko. A number of individuals read and corrected parts of the book in its various stages including Elna Solvang, Sarah Heneghan, Angela Leonard, Christie Harris, and the members of the theology department at Loyola College. Thanks are due as well to the editor of *Analytic Teaching*, Richard Morehouse, for permission to reprint parts of an article I published that appears in chapter 4. I must thank two of my teachers: Abraham J. Malherbe and M. Shawn Copeland. Finally, my wife Mary's love gave me so many ways to rethink the meaning of giving and receiving. I thank her.

Introduction:
Throwing Up in Wynnewood

One of the most delightfully witty passages in Karl Barth's *Church Dogmatics* appears in his defense of angels. After cataloging the opinions of fellow theologians such as Schleiermacher, de Wette, Lipsius, Kaftan, Kirn, Haering, Nitzsch, Seeburg, and Stephan, he says:

> The consensus of all these modern dogmaticians, both among themselves and with their master Schleiermacher, is overwhelming. . . . These modern thinkers are not prepared to take angels seriously. It does not give them the slightest joy to think of them. They are plainly rather peevish and impatient at having to handle the subject. And if we are told in Hebrews 13:2 not to be neglectful of hospitality, since some have entertained angels unawares, these theologians are almost anxiously concerned to refuse angels a lodging in their dogmatics, and think that all things considered they should warn others against extending hospitality to them.[1]

Pity the poor angels! The combination of historical criticism and the demise of the supernatural have left them homeless. Since they have nothing to do with saving faith, the modern theologian considers angels to be as mythical as the fat little *putti* of the High Renaissance artists.

Were Barth alive today and living in America he might also wonder what has happened to hospitality itself. Hospitality, public and private, is under attack from all sides. The term "compassion fatigue" has made its way into our lexicon of societal ills. In an effort to clean up its downtown business district, the city of Atlanta recently considered a zoning ordinance that made not just panhandling illegal but even the act of *giving* money to strangers. Here, in a place perhaps more famous than others for its "southern hospitality," are city elders who seem to despise public generosity. But they are not alone. The current national crisis goes even further. On highways, in shopping malls, and by school yards Americans are encountering strangers with ever-increasing anxiety. Events such as the 9/11 attack, the sniper shootings in Ohio in 2003 and the Washington DC area in 2002, along with the rapid expansion of the Internet, have increased the fear associated with strangers. Our mistrust exhibits itself in a renewed interest in immigration laws and efforts to limit our borders to those who seem to be most like us. Today, protection against strangers and their supposed threat has led us to retinal eye scans, DNA swabbing, and dime-sized details of where we live and work all constantly photographed and recorded by geo-synchronous satellites. Technological palliatives and silicone chips are becoming the sedatives of choice for an increasingly nervous public. Even the United States Patriot Act makes church involvement with strangers, political refugees, and displaced persons such as that promoted by the sanctuary movement in the 1980s hard put. The audacious hospitality of the nineteenth-century abolitionist movement and the Underground Railroad is almost unimaginable today.

The decline of hospitality is because of a number of factors, all of which preceded or are concurrent with the present crisis. Increasing urbanization means that we see more people but we encounter, in the deeper sense, fewer and fewer. The development of political and civic institutions that care for the poor, the orphaned, and the homeless, and ironically, the elimination of the city gate, the place in the past where strangers gathered in expectation of being welcomed and sheltered, also contribute to hospitality's end. The most pernicious factor is the oldest of all: hospitality requires a conscious effort to be "your brother's keeper." As a consequence, we often overlook the fact that being our brother's keeper requires that we give attention to the physical space that we share with others. Hospitality is the caring for that shared space. The hospitable person is making the assertion that when we live or meet together in that space, sometimes permanently and sometimes only momentarily, we strive to keep that space, whether public or private, inviting and welcoming. This is hard to do.

I was once invited to participate in a meeting of second- and third-year college students who had volunteered to serve as mentors for incoming first-year students. The goal of the afternoon was to think through how to help entering students adjust to the academic and social environment of today's college. As part of the session, the volunteers joined in roundtable discussions on issues such as study habits, the honor code, and life in the dorms. Everyone received a set of predetermined questions and my role was to start the conversation, redirect it when needed, and keep it lively. It did not take long for that to happen. One of the questions on life in the dorms raised the following concern: Your mentee complains that every Thursday, Friday, and Saturday night someone has vomited in the elevator. They are tired of this situation. What would you advise them? Why is it a social justice concern?

I have not lived in a dormitory in many years but I take it for granted that puking in public is not a unique event at many colleges. However, the way the question was put, as a concern of social justice, makes me think that it is only raised at a small fraction of colleges across the country. The question was highly appropriate and intended to be taken seriously.

In the discussion that followed, one of the students said that her advice would be to move to a new dorm. Her response is entirely sensible if the first priority of dormitory life is your own comfort and ease. I did not believe then, nor do I believe now, that one has to tolerate distasteful and disgusting behavior. I certainly would not like to live with people who have such little regard for public space and have such a crisis of imagination that they cannot consider expelling their vomitus someplace other than in an elevator. However, avoiding the problem by moving to a new dorm is not a sufficient answer if the goal is to think in a way that is consistent with a desire for social justice, and not least of all, hospitality.

This student's response was not unique. For years, Christians have struggled with how to understand what living in community means. What does it mean to be a guest or a host? How should one respond to strangers, exiles, and the imprisoned? What are the boundaries of my obligations? Are they set by physical or social markers (my house, my street, my family, my country) or are they nondeterminate? These questions are so dogged that it is virtually impossible to find a theologian who has not argued that hospitality was an essential mark of what it means to be Christian.

Tertullian, the third-century theologian, understood and empathized with the plight of women whose nonbelieving husbands insisted on going to the baths when their wives wanted to receive visitors or sneak food to the imprisoned.[2] Pope Gregory the Great (born ca. 540) pulled no punches when he discovered that Janurius, the bishop of Caralis, allowed a monastery to charge a mother for her daughter's burial plot. "This abuse" he says, "which comes from avarice, be not ventured on any more, even in the case of strangers."[3]

In the early modern period, Protestants and Catholics agreed that hospitality was central to the moral life. "Who is my neighbor?" is the crux of Martin Luther's ethics and his "Whether One May Flee from a Deadly Plague" (1527) is typical of the emerging Protestant consensus that the cross demands a love that shows itself in the hospitable treatment of others.[4] The pages of Rembrandt's sketchbooks are filled with drawings of the poor, the lame, and the homeless. His Calvinist background is responsible for this.[5] On the Catholic side, the theological significance of hospitality during the time of the reforms is witnessed to by Ignatius of Loyola (b. 1491) in his *Autobiography*. His story is told as the transformation of a soldier who values honor and despises shame into a pilgrim who suffers beatings, humiliation, and public contempt because he is a traveler, a stranger, and a host. For Ignatius, even temporary lodging such as staying at an inn meant that he had established community with others and a bond that would show itself in hospitality to others. This is seen, for example, in his defense of a mother and daughter who, after being threatened with rape by soldiers at a hostel near Greta, are accompanied by Ignatius on their travels until he falls from exhaustion.

We need not trace the entire history of theological hospitality. The development of the hospital; advances in the penal system; institutions for orphans, immigrants, and refugees all are testament enough of Christian notions of hospitality. Adequate summaries can be found elsewhere.[6] My concern in this book is not with the history of hospitality. Nor am I necessarily concerned with the results or benefits of hospitality, or with outlining or commending certain practices, although each of these is important. My concern is simply with the question, Why should we do this? What is it about Christian theology that compels us to think about hospitality in the first place?

WHAT IS THEOLOGICAL HOSPITALITY?

It is not surprising that the student answered as she did. Teaching about how to live in community with others is not offered with either frequency or urgency. She had not been given, nor had she learned, a good and well-supported understanding of Christian hospitality. I define hospitality in this way:

> In the light of Jesus' life, death, resurrection, and return, Christian hospitality is the intentional, responsible, and caring act of welcoming or visiting, in either public or private places, those who are strangers, enemies, or distressed, without regard for reciprocation.

This definition entails several considerations. First, it resists the popular idea that hospitality is similar to "entertaining." Cultural critics will point out that *Beauty and the Beast* is a classic children's story that helps children confront their natural fear of strangers and helps them imagine the moral consequences of adopting a worldview that gives primacy to loathing, fear, and dread. However, I have to wonder if all of this was diminished when "Be Our Guest" became the signature song for Disney's animated film version of the story and the subsequent advertising campaign for its hotels. At that point, "being our guest" became synonymous with having a good time. The singing plates and dancing forks in the movie give the impression that hospitality toward guests means chasing away frowns, chirping about sunshine, and churning out glee by the gallon. Indeed, the notion of hospitality as entertainment invades most of contemporary society.

Second, Christian hospitality resists an accepted cultural view of gender that sees hospitality as the domain, if not obligation, of women alone. Many of the cultural conflicts of the last forty years can be linked with ease to attempts aimed at overturning images of women as gracious hostesses who made themselves available to the whims and needs of men. Dolores Williams's *Sisters in the Wilderness*, for example, is a searing indictment of how patriarchal and racist theological systems demand service, surrogacy, and submission from African American women.[7] Williams's warning is fair enough. However, I do not believe that we can abandon thinking about hospitality and the ideas associated with it altogether; rather, we must offer a critique of hospitality that is on sure theological footing. As I will show in this book, hospitality is at the very center of what it means to be a Christian and to think theologically.

Third, the reason we do not consider hospitality is that we think too little of responsibility and too much of reciprocity. One corrective to this is found in the papal encyclical *Evangelium Vitae*. Notice how John Paul II tries to reposition the church in regard to society at large.

> A stranger is no longer a stranger for the person who must *become a neighbour* to someone in need, to the point of accepting responsibility for his life, as the parable of the Good Samaritan shows so clearly. Even an enemy ceases to be an enemy for the person who is obliged to love him, to "do good" to him and respond to his immediate needs promptly and with no expectation of repayment.[8]

John Paul is critiquing a popular idea. Many people today have a type of moral karma bank that they feel they must keep replenishing lest they one day find themselves unable to make a withdrawal when they need it the most. A calculation is made to see if they are ahead or behind and how much a particular action is going to count. I want to be clear that Christian thinking about hospitality is something quite different. Hospitality is quickly diluted by concerns for parity and reciprocity; life should not be filtered through the sieve of minimal responsibilities.

Fourth, it is certainly true that ignoring a pool of vomit in an elevator is far less inhospitable than walking on the other side of the road when you encounter a wounded person. Yet, if we cannot act consonant with the gospel in small things, even the inconveniences of life, we will be ill equipped for the larger matters (Luke 16:10). I would dare say that in the student's mind, she was making a distinction between where she *stayed* and where she *lived.* Her staying in the dorm was temporary, much like staying at a hotel. She was not living at home and thus felt no responsibility for any problems other than her own.

Fifth, just as I want my definition of hospitality to resist the idea of entertainment, I want to distinguish it as well from notions of civility and honor. There is little doubt that ancient practices of hospitality were critical in shaping a civil society. As Ladislaus Bolchazy points out, hospitality was influential in helping the ancient Romans move away from xenophobia. In a society where strangers were viewed as having magical powers that could be used as weapons, individual hospitality was a means of disarming the stranger and warding off evil. As Roman law advanced, hospitality was often a diplomatic tool used to prevent hostility and a means of transforming strangers into political allies. This opened the way to view hospitality as a civilizing concept, and it became a virtue commended by the Stoics.[9] Yet, although the New Testament shows the influence of Greek and Roman moral philosophy, the early Christian practice of hospitality was a profession of faith in the rule of God—being useful to Caesar was secondary.

Some cultures (ancient and modern) practice hospitality as a matter of honor.[10] Abraham's reception of the three strangers in Genesis 18 is a portrayal of what happens when the hospitality rituals of nomads are upheld; the violence of Genesis 19 shows what happens when they are broken. The concept of hospitality as honor appears in the New Testament as well. Jesus' castigation of Simon for not offering him a kiss, water, and oil reveals the expectations that the conventions of hospitality would be upheld, but the larger point that Jesus makes of the incident is about forgiveness and not about manners (Luke 7).

SHEEP ON THE RIGHT, GOATS ON THE LEFT

The goal of this book is to present hospitality from the point of view of systematic theology. The framework is the passage in Matthew 25:31-46, the parable of the sheep and the goats. In this passage Jesus pictures the Last Judgment as a time in which the Son of Man will answer interrogatives about why some will be accepted into the kingdom and others will be banished. The answer he gives is that admission is based on care for the hungry, the thirsty, the stranger, the naked, the sick, and the imprisoned. In this book I connect several of those terms (strangers, enemies, guests, and prisoners) with particular theological doctrines (Christology, reconciliation, ecclesiology, and eschatology) and with a select group of theologians and social philosophers. I want to show that hospitality is not simply the practice of a virtue but is fundamental to Christianity's understanding of God, self, and the world.

I can expect criticism that the center of any theological text on hospitality ought to have reflections on the Eucharist. It will be argued that the banquet of the Lord is the fullest expression of God's hospitality toward us. There is little that can be said to refute this. It was in "the breaking of the bread" that Jesus was made known to the disciples at Emmaus (Luke 24). Yet, because this connection seems so obvious, I have chosen to approach the Eucharist in ways that are more oblique than direct in the hope that the reader's own and better reflections will emerge. A second, and perhaps equally worrisome, objection will be that I have not emphasized hospitality and the church's mission of evangelism enough. Again, this seems second nature to me and I hope to my readers as well. The entire point of hospitality is that

Christians are a people *in* the world and *for* the world. Indeed, the four doctrines I have selected should be viewed as consanguineous with church mission.

Another possible objection concerns the meaning of the phrase "the least of these my brethren" in Matthew 25:40 (RSV). Who are they? There are two possible interpretations. On the one hand, Jesus could have been referring to "the least" as those who were disciples. Those who were imprisoned, the naked, the stranger, might be fairly interpreted as those disciples who were either persecuted or suffering from the unfortunate conditions of life. If this is the case, then the command to care for "the least of these my brethren" would be limited.

There is some merit to this interpretation. For example, Jesus' commission to the apostles as they leave him in Matthew 10 is a handbook on how they are to act as strangers and guests among those to whom they preach. On being received into someone's home, they are to "greet" it, give their blessing of peace, not shop around for more comfortable arrangements, and not dawdle where they are rejected. They are to keep in mind that a judgment worse than what fell upon Sodom and Gomorrah awaits the inhospitable host. Moreover, Jesus envisions that the messenger's message will divide households, a fact that would make their hospitable welcome suspect in the first place (Matthew 10:34-36). The entire passage stresses that discipleship means enduring persecution and rejection: betrayal, denunciation, and beating were not to be surprises to them but seals of their witness.

Statements like these make it possible that the early church read their own current postresurrection experiences back into the preresurrection preaching of Jesus, a possibility strengthened at least by the fact that we have little evidence of the disciples actually being treated this way in the Gospels during the lifetime of Jesus. In fact, the one clear case in which the disciples were so mistreated, so much so that they wanted to "call down fire" upon the residents of Samaria, is actually about the rejection of Jesus himself (Luke 9:51-56). Be that as it may, what is clear is that welcoming "a prophet," welcoming a "righteous person" in

Matthew 10:40-41, brings with it a reward of like kind. The parallelisms in the early part of the passage would lead us to believe that "the disciples" and "the little ones" of Matthew 10:42 are also to be considered one and the same.

On the other hand, "the brethren" may not be the disciples of Jesus or members of the early church at all. The criteria listed for acceptance or rejection by the King in Matthew 25:31-45 is not the faith status of either *the giver* or *the receiver* of compassion. This is a more inclusive reading of the parable than the first alternative and the one that I adopt in this book. I hold it to be the case that "the least of these my brethren" refers to anyone, believer or not, who lives in some condition of peril. Like Jesus, we ought to worry less about who needs compassion and more about how to get it to them.

Chapter One

"Poor, Wayfaring Stranger"

CHRIST, THURMAN, DU BOIS, AND THE SPIRITUALS

In April of 1947, Howard Thurman became the first African American to deliver the Ingersoll Lectures at Harvard Divinity School. His lecture put him in the company of William James, Josiah Royce, Edgar Sheffield Brightman, William Ernest Hocking, and Alfred North Whitehead. Thurman had much in common with his predecessors, particularly his affinity for the philosophy of pragmatism.[1] It was Thurman's belief that there had bloomed on American soil a view of life, of the human condition, and of truth that was centered in just the type of raw approach to human experience that those other fellows had advocated. He said, "The human spirit is so involved in the endless cycle of birth, of living and dying, that in some sense each man is an authority, a key interpreter of the meaning of the totality of the experience."[2] This could have been said by any of the American pragmatists. Where Thurman parted company with them, however, was in his decision to reach back to the Negro spiritual as a resource for understanding these matters. He announces that he has chosen the Negro spirituals as his subject because in many ways they are "the voice, sometimes strident, sometimes muted and weary, of a people for whom the cup of suffering overflowed in haunting tones of majesty, beauty and power!"[3] The intellectual challenge of the songs was not their unusual meter, "the real significance of the songs . . . is revealed at a deeper level of experience, in the ebb and flow of the tides that feed the rivers of man's thinking and aspiring."[4] In speaking this way Thurman was asserting like W. E. B. Du Bois that Negro sacred songs about Jesus and Christianity were fundamental in understanding the Negro's experience in America. The spirituals' repeated focus on an individual's wilderness, wandering, and welcome is done in the light of an interpretation of Christ as a poor, wayfaring stranger who took on the totality of human existence.[5]

We should be reminded of this if we are interested in seeing how the songs are helpful in constructing a theology of hospitality and a Christology of hospitality in particular. Thurman helps us remember that we ought to start with the assertion that Jesus himself appeared to folk in the towns and villages of Palestine *as a homeless stranger.* As charismatic, challenging, and convincing as he was in preaching his vision of the reign of God, at the end of the day the saying still applied: "Foxes have holes and birds of the air have nests, but the Son of Man has no place to lay his head" (Matthew 8:20 NIV). Our presumption of familiarity with the Gospel narratives makes the full significance of this difficult to remember. Too often insight into the humanity of Jesus is either underweighted or overlooked. Reminders and explications of how Jesus lived (his person; that is, his divine and human natures) are important because they are the foundation for understanding what Jesus does (his work of redemption). Any attempt to construct a Christology must keep in mind that once Jesus began his mission, there is no indication that he ever stayed under his own roof again. When this is done, it underscores the importance of hospitality for those who would be his disciples.

The Gospel writers ask the reader to develop not just a remembrance of the facts of his homelessness but also to develop empathy for Jesus' plight. By feeling for Jesus, the reader gains insight into Jesus' own empathy with the distressed of this world and his gifts of hospitality toward them. His empathy for the homeless shows in his healing of the demon-possessed man from Gerasene (Mark 5:1-20). His empathy for the homeless explains his detestation of those who exploit the widow and leave her without shelter (Matthew 23:14).[6] His generosity welcomes the despised to eat bread with him (Luke 19:1-10).

The Gospels show Jesus' empathy for the imprisoned by stressing how his own actions consistently put him on the edge of arrest. He speaks of prison as a matter of course, as a capricious fact of daily life (Matthew 5:21-26; 18:29-31). Indeed, life in occupied Palestine meant living with harassment from civil authorities and adjusting to those who could confront, compel, and convict (Matthew 5:39-41). The threat of imprisonment was so much on his mind that he uses it to illustrate the justice and mercy of God toward the forgiven and the unforgiving (Matthew 18:21-35).

As for clothing, the evangelists draw upon a series of sayings by Jesus that stress the peril of nakedness and show that Jesus knew of the anxiety it brought. "And why do you worry about clothing? Consider the lilies of the field, how they grow; they neither toil nor spin, yet I tell you, even Solomon in all his glory was not clothed like one of these. But if God so clothes the grass of the field, which is alive today and tomorrow is thrown into the oven, will he not much more clothe you—you of little faith?" (Matthew 6:28-31). Indeed, the risk of being without clothing is transformed into a mark of discipleship (Matthew 5:40) and Gospel writers emphasize the loss of Jesus' clothes during his arrest, trial, and crucifixion: "they stripped him" (Matthew 27:28) and "divided his clothes among them" (Mark 15:24).

Similarly, the hunger of Jesus is a prominent feature of the Gospels. Although the temptation narrative is the most often recalled scene in this regard, Jesus knows the hunger of the weary crowd and has compassion upon them in Matthew 15:32. When he is hungry he looks for figs and is short with anger when nothing is found (Matthew 21:18-19). He justifies his actions in gleaning grain from another's field by appealing to the action of David's men (Matthew 12:3). His thirst on the cross in Jerusalem, perhaps the penultimate mark of his humanity (John 19:28), is foreshadowed by his thirst on the road through Samaria (John 4:7).

These experiences are important because they make clear that Jesus is depicted not as just saying the words "I was hungry and you gave me something to eat, I was thirsty and you gave me something to drink, I was a stranger and you invited me in, I needed clothes and you clothed me, I was sick and you looked after me, I was in prison and you came to visit me" (Matthew 25:34-36 NIV), but of having actually lived them. The Gospels want to ensure that Jesus' humanity is seen as whole, complete, and total. It is what allows us to understand hospitality as an aspect of Christology. To the degree that we understand Jesus as a homeless stranger we will understand the parameters of the problem, What does it mean to welcome those who wander among us?

African American Sacred Songs: Their Origin, Development, and Christology

Although it is common to call all of the African American religious songs that emerged from the era of slavery up to the arrival of "gospel" music in the 1930s "spirituals," the early catalogers of the spirituals made distinctions between types of spirituals, calling a portion of them "the sorrow songs."[7] John Wesley Work Jr., for example, in his 1915 book *Folk Song of the American Negro*, makes this division and noted that "there are two extremes of emotion,—joy and sorrow—expressed in this music. There is practically no middle ground."[8]

The spirituals cannot be separated from the fact that they were essentially work songs, meant to provide relief from the tedium of mindless and backbreaking labor. The easily repeated refrains, the reliance upon call and response, and the use of first-person pronouns all indicate that the songs were intended to give reprieve, build community, and provide an assurance that the work they did in no way defined who they were. The songs that slaves sang "in church," that is, in organized gatherings during times of worship, were often quite different: they sang the hymns and tunes of John and Charles Wesley and Isaac Watts. This accounts in part for the difficulty the early choirmasters of historically black colleges such as Fisk, Howard, and Hampton had in getting permission to have the songs performed in chapel and church. It was only after the songs were arranged along the lines of the European concert tradition that they became "spiritual" despite their message of Jesus, faith, and redemption. This bias was a matter of class and supposed sophistication. Some were embarrassed by these field songs and saw them as the signatures of an undereducated and often illiterate people.

However, this view portrays a slighting of an essential fact. All music in traditional African culture is spiritual. The African lives in a spiritual world, and music is a part of everyday life, and in particular, a life of work. The spirituals emerged not just because of slavery, but because the slaves were working people surrounded by the preaching and teaching of the gospel. Had the dominant religion in the era of slavery been something other than Christian, the slaves would have adapted their music to that just as easily.[9]

The spirituals often contain remnants of African tribal religion. This appears, for example, in the repeated references found in the spirituals to Old Testament figures such as Daniel, Moses, and Jacob. The creators of the spirituals knew the biblical narratives, and they knew the importance of ancestors in African religion. Daniel, Moses, and Jacob became not just figures caught in the pages of the past but living and active participants, even protectors, in the present who could be appealed to for survival, resilience, and resistance. In the song "The Social Band," Mary the mother of Jesus is pleaded for:

Bright angels on the water,
Hovering by the light;
Poor sinner standing in darkness
And cannot see the light.

I want Aunty Mary to go with me,
I want Aunty Mary to go with me,
I want Aunty Mary to go with me,
To join the social band.[10]

Slave religion was highly fluid and syncretic. This explains the relative ease by which some slaves adopted Catholicism. The appeal of rites and rituals, the prominence given to the saints and to Mary, and the general aura of the sacredness of daily life (as opposed to the dichotomy between Sunday and the rest of the week often prominent in Protestant worship) facilitated the ease with which some slaves turned to Catholicism. The fluid and imaginative nature of popular Catholicism might be the reason in the song "Sister Mary Had-a But One Child" an angel is given feminine gender:

Sister angel appeared to Joseph,
And gave him-a this-a command,
"Arise ye, take your wife and child,
Go flee into Egypt land."[11]

Yet, despite the tendency toward syncretism, the spirituals are decidedly monotheistic:

Someday Peter and someday Paul,
    The angels are watching over me—
Ain't but one God made us all,
    The angels are watching over me—[12]

Whereas Catholicism contributed dynamism to the songs, the influence of a taut Calvinism in early Afro-Baptist theology is perhaps reflected in songs that speak of the immutability of God as a comfort to believers:

God is a God!
God don't never change!
God is a God,
And He always will be God!

The earth's His footstool and heaven's his throne,
The whole creation, all His own,
His love and power will prevail,
His promises will never fail, saying,

God is a God!
God don't never change!
God is a God,
And He always will be God![13]

The introduction of Christianity into slave life was both gradual and steady. Most of the slaves brought to the New World were young and could be poor bearers of the traditions of their parents. When the United States passed legislation that banned the importation of slaves in 1807, the traditions of the elders fell on hard times. As the memory of their religious past faded, Christianity filled the void.[14] Yet, there is evidence that some themes are so often repeated that the spirituals seem to be almost at one with Augustinian and medieval notions of *homo viator*.[15] This concept, "wandering man," appears, for example, in Augustine's *Confessions*, where humans are often seen as wanderers in this world ever searching for a home. Travel by foot was paradigmatic of religious seekers during the Middle Ages and this type of travel became a metaphor for the misery of life. Sentiments of either or both types can be seen in the classic spiritual:

Sometimes I feel like a motherless child,
Sometimes I feel like a motherless child,
Sometimes I feel like a motherless child,
A long way from home,
A long way from home,
True believer;
A long way from home.[16]

The wandering life of Jesus and his followers is punctuated in the spirituals by references to travel, pilgrimage, and restlessness—with the distinction, of course, that the end of the journey could also be viewed as liberation from slavery and not necessarily travel to the Holy City of Jerusalem or heaven above. Wading in the water, crossing Jordan, and going home all functioned as code words for escape north. When the double entendre does not appear, the emphasis is on the wanderer's experience of the absolute misery of this world.

> I am a poor, wayfaring stranger,
> While journeying through this world of woe,
> Yet there's no sickness, toil, and danger,
> In that bright world to which I go;
> I'm going there to see my father,
> I'm going there no more to roam,
> I'm just a going over Jordan,
> I'm just going over home.[17]

Hope, relief from this world, is found in *imatio Christi:*

> The foxes, they have holes in the ground,
> The birds have nests in the air,
> The Christians have a hiding place,
> But sinners ain't got nowhere.
> Now ain't them hard trials, great tribulations?[18]

These references show that the spirituals uniformly affirm the humanity of Jesus in the Gospels; the "fundamentals of the faith," the death, burial, and resurrection of Jesus are taken directly from 1 Corinthians 15. The songs are not just traditional but are heralds of tradition. In these matters and many more the spirituals show themselves as continuous with the mainstream of Christian doctrine. However, relatively few of the songs are directly trinitarian in outlook. As Bruno Chenu says:

> The spirituals do not demonstrate a reflective Trinitarian theology. Only rarely is Jesus designated as the "only Son" or as the "darlin' Son." To my knowledge, only one text speaks of the Father-Son relationship: "The Father looked at His Son an' smiled, The Son did look at-a Him."[19]

If the measure of how trinitarian the spirituals are is a matter of counting the references to Father and Son in the same song then perhaps Chenu's point is well taken. But is it the case that the writers of the spirituals were naive and unsophisticated in regard to Christology? Thurman wrote before Chenu: "For the most part, a very simple theory of the incarnation is ever present. The simpler assumptions of Christian orthodoxy are utilized. There was no elaborate scheme of separate office and function between God and Jesus and only a very rare reference to the Holy Spirit."[20] Or asked another way: Did the writers of the spirituals oppose trinitarian thought and thereby deliberately choose to exclude references to Jesus as the Son of God?[21] Are we dealing with songs that are so impromptu and circumstantial that we should not expect them to reflect the precise language of the Nicene and Chalcedonian Creeds? If this proves to be the case, then the spirituals may be lacking as adequate reflections on Christology and thereby not be fully helpful in understanding the theological basis of hospitality.

Suitable explanations to these questions are unearthed when it is considered how the spirituals originated, how they were repeated, and how they were collected. As for the origins of the songs, it must be understood that the writers of the spirituals were under a number of influences—the African influence has been noted already. Whereas some musicologists and ethnologists have been able to document how some songs were sung in certain regions of the country at the time in which they were heard, for the large part those songs had been passed down orally and rarely in written form. As a result, the songs have a number of variants for the same sort of reasons that baffle historical critics in their study of the Gospels. The indigenous nature of the songs, as a truly American art form, only helps obscure their origins. It is the nature of folk songs to be pithy, repetitious, and written in shorthand.

In the second place, slaves were catechized in the most rudimentary way. Catechesis among the slaves, though often little more than exercises of rote memory, was time-consuming— a luxury the slaves neither had nor masters were willing to offer. Preachers to slaves focused not on the Trinity (or matters of doctrine beyond those directly related to regeneration) but on admonitions, particularly those of the apostle Paul, which urged obedience and submission.

Third, and most important of all, the theological background of the writers of the spirituals came from a number of strands. Baptists, Methodists, Presbyterians, and Episcopalians were all slaveholders and their theology and polity dominated the religious atmosphere of the South. Thus, the spirituals were not made from one whole theological cloth, by one school, in one era; the songs were the result of complex circumstances and multiple theological dispositions. The Quakers would have been on one end of the spectrum of Christological influences upon the slaves. The Society's efforts in evangelism and abolition influenced a significant number of the freed slaves. It is reasonable to assume then that some aspects of Quaker theology influenced the texts of African American sacred songs. The Quakers were divided over the Trinity and held at least three different positions.[22] Similarly, the Unitarians were also active in the abolitionist movement and their dissent from orthodox Christology is well known. In fact, since some of the songs have their roots in the time when deism held sway, blacks, slave or free, who sat in the balconies in church services where the preacher was under the influence of the Enlightenment, may or may not have been exposed to any more of a "high Christology" than the whites who sat on the first floor of the sanctuary. At the other end of the spectrum was the influence of John Wesley. His Christology, according to some interpreters, appears to blend the Western emphasis on juridical atonement with an Eastern emphasis on deification—human participation in the divine nature.[23]

Thus, it may be held that the composers of the spirituals were not deliberate in excluding references to the Trinity, but rather brought the Trinity and Christology into songs when affirmations of both the full humanity and the full deity of Jesus Christ fit the lyrical thesis of the songs. This is evident in the lyrics of simple songs such as this:

He's a mighty good leader,
He's a mighty good leader. . . .
Jesus Christ, God's Son, God's Son,
He's a mighty good leader.[24]

There are songs that affirm the preexistence of Christ and the *communicatio idiomatum,* the doctrine proposing that the attributes of both the divine and human natures are ascribed to the one person of Jesus.[25] In the following song, notice how Jesus is deemed as both Creator and Redeemer:

This is the Man who made this earth,
This is the Man—
This is the Man who died for you,
This is the Man—[26]

There is one creative song that celebrates the two natures of Jesus Christ and the *kenosis,* or the self-emptying of the second person of the Trinity, by drawing upon images found in the book of Revelation:

John saw the heavens open,
The Conqueror riding down,
He looked and saw white horses;
And rider following on.
If you want to know the Conqueror,
He is the word of God,
His eyes are like a burning throne,
He is the word of God.
Hosanna to the Prince of Life,
Who clothed Himself in clay,
And entered the iron gate of death,
And bore the ties away.
See how the conqueror mounts aloft.
And to his Father flies.
With scars of honor on His flesh,
And trails in His eyes.[27]

We should not forget that the bulk of the songs stress the humanity of Jesus, and it is my contention that this is exactly what made the spirituals so popular and why they attracted the attention of African Americans even after slavery was ended. The repeated stress upon Jesus' homelessness, his suffering, and his being misunderstood resonated with the totality of the African American experience. It also explains why W. E. B. Du Bois, a man who was often at odds with religious, intellectual, and political sentiments of his day, found them so appealing.

W. E. B. Du Bois and the Sorrow Songs

For Du Bois, the spirituals, "the Sorrow Songs" as he called them, were important critiques of American aesthetics. He writes:

> Little of beauty has America given the world save the rude grandeur God himself stamped on her bosom; the human spirit in this new world has expressed itself in vigor and ingenuity rather than in beauty. And so by fateful chance the Negro folk-song—the rhythmic cry of the slave—stands to-day not simply as the sole American music, but as the most beautiful expression of human experience born this side the seas. It has been neglected, it has been, and is, half despised, and above all it has been persistently mistaken and misunderstood; but notwithstanding, it still remains as the singular spiritual heritage of the nation and the greatest gift of the Negro people.[28]

This critique of American aesthetics highlights the fact that Du Bois consistently feels that African Americans are a misunderstood people. They are misunderstood because they appear as a people out of place. They are strangers in their own country. In the opening chapter of *The Souls of Black Folk*, Du Bois gives voice to a young man who cries out "Why did God make me an outcast and a stranger in mine own house?"[29] The question is both an accusation and a lament, resonant with the Psalms and Lamentations in the Bible. Typically, the question is understood as an explication of Du Bois's notion of what he called "double consciousness"—the feeling that one is both "Negro and an American" and that this tension is never fully resolved. However, the question of the young man, this cry of the stranger, is part of a motif used by Du Bois not only within *The Souls of Black Folk* but also across the collection of his writing, highlighting Du Bois's fusing of his objective observations as a sociologist with his own experiences with social fragmentation. My reading of Du Bois suggests that his interpretation of the spirituals is his attempt to make plain his answer to the question of the young man, to himself, and to white America.

In *The Souls of Black Folk* Du Bois relies upon a cluster of ideas in describing black folk as strangers; he uses outcasts, exiles, vagabonds, the helpless, and the pitiable. Descriptions are given of the chance and fearful encounter with the wandering migrant and the homeless refugee. What ties them together into a single motif is that they are depictions of a person or group whose appearance as a stranger is disconcerting and confusing to others; they cause consternation and discomfort in those who encounter them. Even when Du Bois is simply reciting the facts and statistics associated with the Freedmen's Bureau, he cannot help but include in his observations how the freed blacks are viewed as persons: they are seen as a mass of strangers and fugitives that fluster the North and cause the South to fume.[30]

From a literary perspective, Du Bois, in the preface, invites the reader to visit a world, to step within "the Veil," and see what they have not seen before. As an invitation, it is an act of hospitality. It is the position of host toward guest. As such, it is the position that authors often take toward readers, particularly in the more genteel literary world from which Du Bois wrote. And then in an act of even greater generosity, he tells us that he has included at the head of each chapter a melody, a bar of music from the "Sorrow Songs."

Yet after this invitation, Du Bois deliberately positions the Sorrow Songs as a paradox. The paradox begins with the epigrams at the start of each chapter. They are bits of poetry or prose, typically lines that are redolent, mournful, and familiar words from the white literary world of Arthur Symons, A. C. Swinburne, James Russell Lowell, Lord Byron, Friedrich Schiller, and John Greenleaf Whittier. Because the words are visible on the page, we can understand them. The paradox, however, is that Du Bois only gives the musical notes to the Sorrow Songs that compose the other half of the epigrams. He does not give any explanation of the musical notes, their origin, title, or author. The bars of music stand alone. To understand the melodies requires two acts. First, one has to be able to read music, a feat that excludes many people, and second, one has to be able to place the melody with words. For most people, then, the music remains hidden and strange. The effect of this paradox is startling: Du Bois has indicated that the world that he intends to explain is indeed hidden and elusive. The bars of music are foreign and strange and are the rhythms of a people who are foreign and strange. The music is a type of riddle much like the riddle of the Sphinx, or of Africa as a whole, which Du Bois points to in the essay "Of the Wings of Atalanta."[31] Blacks are strangers in America whose voices are clear to those who have lived within the Veil but muted to those who have lived without.

The conclusion of *The Souls of Black Folk* ends with the "The Sorrow Songs," a detailed explanation of the sources and meanings of the melodies that were hidden to us at the start of the book. Now, at last, we are given both music and words. He explains his selections as "ten master songs," which are "the music of an unhappy people, of the children of disappointment; they tell us of death and suffering and unvoiced longing toward a truer world, of misty wanderings and hidden ways."[32] Du Bois points out how the songs are the words of "trouble and exile" of "the fugitive and weary wanderer." Still, something else needs to be noted. The epigram at the start of the essay is credited as a "Negro Song." Why? The author is not noted because the authors of the Sorrow Songs are anonymous strangers, like blacks in America.

Du Bois makes use of this revealed yet hidden aspect of the stranger motif when he writes his eulogy for Alexander Crummell (1819–98), the missionary, intellectual, and educator whose black nationalist and Pan African speeches and activism stirred Europe, America, and Africa alike. After explaining how Crummell overcame hate, despair, doubt, and humiliation, he says:

He did his work,—he did it nobly and well; and yet I sorrow that here he worked alone, with so little human sympathy. His name to-day, in this broad land, means little, and comes to fifty million ears laden with no incense of memory or emulation. And herein lies the tragedy of the age: not that men are poor,—all men know something of poverty; not that men are wicked, who is good? not that men are ignorant,—what is Truth? Nay, that men know so little of men.[33]

Du Bois combines hearing, memory, and ignorance to point out that just as white America knows nothing of the riddle of the Sorrow Songs, so also they know nothing of Crummell as a man. He remains a stranger.

The contrast between knowing and not knowing is a technique that Du Bois used throughout his life. In Du Bois's 1919 essay "The Souls of White Folk" he says:

Of them I am singularly clairvoyant. I see in and through them. I view them from unusual points of vantage. Not as a foreigner do I come, for I am native, not foreign, bone of their thought and flesh of their language. Mine is not the knowledge of the traveler or the colonial composite of dear memories, words and wonder. . . . Rather I see these souls undressed and from the back and side. I see the working of their entrails. I know their thoughts and they know that I know.[34]

In this passage the motif of the stranger is put to use to show that Du Bois has particular insight. In an era where the black body was stripped and naked and the white body hidden and clothed, here the white body is laid more than bare, it is penetrated and cut open like a cadaver. His knowledge of whites is of closest intimacy. The knowledge that whites have of blacks is foggy, cloudy, and in the realm of the hidden.

The more a person travels the more a person becomes aware of their sense of self and their sense of the world. Travel brings us to consciousness because we are removed from the familiar and set toward the undiscovered. Travel, of course, is often enough a pragmatic activity: getting from here to there might be all that we consider. However, even on this level, travel fundamentally increases the likelihood of either being a stranger or encountering a stranger. To travel is to risk this encounter and the resultant reordering of our sense of self and other. This, too, becomes part of Du Bois's interpretation of the spirituals.

Du Bois's writings indicate that he walked in the foothills of Massachusetts, mounted a horse in the pursuit of a teaching position in Tennessee, rode streetcars in Nashville, and boarded trains in countries across Europe. In the essay "The Meaning of Progress" found in *The Souls of Black Folk,* Du Bois narrates his summer search for a teaching position. Upon leaving the Teacher's Institute, he tells us that he traveled first by foot, because horses were too expensive, into the wilderness of Tennessee. The passage is striking because he paints a picture of entering into the end of civilization. He wanders "beyond railways, beyond stage lines, to a land of 'varmints' and rattlesnakes, where the coming of a stranger was an event." [35] In the following pages, Du Bois remembers with some delight the wonder of this first teaching position, despite his encounters with the persistence of racism, ignorance, and poverty. In the second part of the essay, Du Bois says that he returned to the small village ten years later out of a longing to learn how life had gone for his former pupils. The report is not encouraging. Some students have died; another was almost lynched. A husband has beaten to death a young wife. Yet, in a few ways he sees progress: a heavy crop, an expanded chalkboard, reports of some folk "doing well."

The contrast of these two experiences makes Du Bois reflect on the meaning of progress. He writes:

> My journey was done, and behind me lay hill and dale, and Life and Death. How shall man measure Progress there where the dark-faced Josie lies? How many heartfuls of sorrow shall balance a bushel of wheat? How hard a thing is life to the lowly, and yet how human and real! And all this life and love and strife and failure,—is it the twilight of nightfall or the flush of some faint-dawning day? Thus sadly musing, I rode to Nashville in the Jim Crow car.[36]

Two points are worth noting. First, travel has made him weary. But it is not just the weariness of uncomfortable seating; it is the weariness that comes from examining life. Although he now has a better position and brighter prospects than he did when he was young and adventurous, there has been no progress for his schoolchildren and this is a heavy weight on his shoulder. The schoolmaster has prospered but not his pupils. Second, we should see that whereas ten years earlier he had walked into the village, now, at the end of his journey, he says that he rode back on the train. Progress, if measured by only economic and technological standards, has increased. Yet, this too proves to be a paradox: his musings occur in the segregated railcar. What we have then is, in literary terms, an *inclusio:* he walks in, but rides the train out. This is a sign of increasing industrial progress and his own increased wealth, yet in both cases the journey is underscored by the reality of racism made apparent by the Jim Crow laws. Nothing in America reminded blacks of their status as an "other" more than these laws that regulated every form of public and private hospitality.

Reflection on weariness often produces anger. As David Levering Lewis points out, Du Bois was outraged by the treatment he received while traveling from Atlanta to Savannah to prepare for the Paris Exposition of 1900 and, after encouragement from Booker T. Washington, fired off an angry letter to the Southern Railway.[37] However, there is evidence that Du Bois was publicly attacking the Jim Crow laws at least a year earlier, and he did so because the laws engendered animosity toward strangers. Writing for the *Independent* in March 1899, under the caption "The Negro and Crime," Du Bois writes:

> Finally, the last cause of Negro crime is the exaggerated and unnatural separation in the South of the best classes of whites and blacks. A drawing of the color line, that extends to street-cars, elevators and cemeteries, which leaves no common ground of meeting, no medium of communication, no ties of sympathy between two races who live together and whose interests are at bottom one—such a discrimination is more than silly, it is dangerous. It

makes it possible for the mass of whites to misinterpret the aims and aspiration of the Negroes, to mistake self-reliance for insolence, and condemnation of lynch-law for sympathy with crime. It makes it possible for the Negroes to believe that the best people of the South hate and despise them, and express their antipathy in proscribing them, taunting them and crucifying them. Such terrible misapprehensions are false, and the sooner some way is made by which the best elements of both races can sympathize with each other's struggles and in a calm Christian spirit discuss them together—the sooner such conferences can take place all over the South, the sooner the lynch-law will disappear and crime be abated.[38]

Notice here how Du Bois has deftly tied together public inhospitality with the exclusion of opportunities to meet the stranger, the other, on some common ground. The inability to ride together in a train means that the two races are unable to find a way to discover each other's basic humanity. Moreover, it leads directly to violence.

Public inhospitality—and the violence that accompanied it—to black strangers in America did not go unnoticed in Germany, and the German government made propaganda out of it during the First World War. Du Bois, writing for *The Crisis* in March of 1919, recalls a flyer dropped by a German balloon in September of 1918. The message read in part:

Hello, boys, what are you doing over here? Fighting the Germans? Why? Have they ever done you any harm ? . . . What is democracy? Personal freedom, all citizens enjoying the same rights socially and before the law. Do you enjoy the same rights as the white people do in America . . . ? Can you go into a restaurant where white people dine? Can you get a seat in the theatre where white people sit? Can you can get a seat or a berth in the railroad car, or can you even ride in the South in the same street car with white people? And how about the law? Is lynching and the most horrible crimes connected therewith, a lawful proceeding in a democratic country? Now all this is entirely different in Germany, where they do like colored people, where they treat them as gentlemen and as white men and quite a number of colored people have fine positions in business in Berlin and other German cities.[39]

The opening, "Hello, boys," rings to American ears as one of our standard racial epithets. I would suggest, however, that the expression should be understood as shorthand for "doughboys." Less excusable is the fact that the flyer overlooks Germany's own practices and attitudes; this was the era of colonialism and social science. However, what is most important to see is that the intent is to cause Negro soldiers to reflect upon their own mistreatment in public accommodations. To incite desertion, the Germans pointed out how the violation of the public space is founded on violence toward strangers.

Du Bois did not need the Germans to remind him of this. It was already burned within him. So deep was his animosity toward segregated rail travel that even the most common of human touches startle Du Bois's piety. In his editorial for *The Crisis* in August of 1921, notice how he finds himself nourished by the kindness of strangers:

> I confess I was suspicious of Hopkinsville. I couldn't find it on the map, and I knew no one who knew it. It took twelve hours of "Jim Crow" to reach it from Cincinnati. But it was worth it. It was worth twelve hours of wakefulness, three in a seat, to see the Woman approach. She was buxom, sweet, fair and golden of skin, and she had a little thin baby in her arms.
>
> "How's your baby?" asked a traveler.
>
> "It ain't mine," she answered blithely, "that poor woman yonder is traveling with four and I just took this one to 'tend for her."
>
> Can you beat it? Are we not the sweetest-souled people in America? Imagine any other brand of American female voluntarily taking the mewling, scrawny infant of a poor stranger and sitting up with it all night in the worst "Jim Crow" car of Louisville and Nashville railroad, just because the poor mother "had four"! It chastened my withered soul. I was glad to let a woman and a tired boy crowd on me and sit half on my knees while I sat happily and talked with God.[40]

Du Bois's repeated experiences with being a stranger are heightened by his knowledge of biblical narratives: he knows passages that show both the joy of welcome and sourness of inhospitality. We can trace this by turning to the essay "Of the Quest of the Golden Fleece." He writes of how "a black stranger in Baker County, Georgia, for instance, is liable to be stopped anywhere on the public highway and made to state his business to the satisfaction of any white interrogator. If he fails to give a suitable answer, or seems too independent or 'sassy,' he may be arrested or summarily driven away."[41] Here we have a case of driving a mule wagon while black.

Outside of *The Souls of Black Folk,* Du Bois often ties the ill reception of the black stranger to the parable of the sheep and the goats in Matthew 25. An early interpretation is found in the 1911 short story "Jesus Christ in Georgia." An even more biting essay, "Jesus Christ in Baltimore," came out the same year. Du Bois returned to the idea again in 1920 with "Jesus Christ in Texas." Similar ideas are found in "The Gospel according to Mary Brown" (1919), "Pontius Pilate" (1920), and "The Son of God" (1933).[42]

In "Jesus Christ in Georgia," Jesus appears as a stranger who is invited to dinner by his white host who does not know the stranger's real identity. However, the black servant, a butler pouring tea, recognizes the stranger as Jesus and falls prostrate before him crying out, "My Lord and My God!" Du Bois fuses two narratives from the Gospels, the recognition of the risen Jesus by Thomas (John 20:24-28) and the recognition of the risen Jesus by the disciples on the road to Emmaus where Jesus is made known "in the breaking of the bread." (Luke 24:30-35) The story moves through a series of recognitions and half-recognitions: the identity of the stranger is once again hidden from a rector who, stumbling to recall where he has seen this stranger before, says, "Surely I know you; I have met you somewhere. . . . You—remember me, do you not?" To which the stranger replies, "I never knew you."[43] Du Bois has this same stranger practice hospitality to a runaway convict: he gives him water, washes him, and takes the chains off his feet. The convict, struggling to make sense of this, says to the stranger, "Why you'se a nigger, too."[44] The third recognition comes at the end of the story when a farmer's wife sees the lynched body of the convict after he has been falsely accused of assaulting her. As she looks, the body of the convict is transformed into that of the stranger, and the tree takes the form of a cross. She sees the stranger as the body of the tortured Christ. In this story we have a picture of Du Bois's complete and absolute identification of Jesus' humanity with the misrepresentation and suffering of black folk.

It is apparent that Du Bois, and Thurman after him, saw the spirituals as the reflections of a particular people upon a universal condition: strangeness. Whereas they both affirm that this is the essential condition of African American people, they also propose that this is the condition of particular persons, and no one more so than Jesus, the poor, wayfaring stranger from Nazareth. As such, these reflections on Jesus' humanity serve as a valuable resource for the construction of a Christology of hospitality. When these reflections are taken to heart, they go a considerable way toward helping us understand our own essential loneliness, isolation, and search for a hospitable community. If we fail to see the direct link between Christology and hospitality, we run the danger of being confronted with the opening of the Gospel of John:

> He was in the world, and though the world was made through him, the world did not recognize him. He came to that which was his own, but his own did not receive him. Yet to all who received him, to those who believed in his name, he gave the right to become children of God (John 1:10-12 NIV).

Chapter Two

The Death of Hostility

STRANGERS, ENEMIES, AND RECONCILIATION

Although Jesus asks his disciples to love their enemies, the parable of the sheep and the goats does not mention enemies as the recipients of hospitality. Nevertheless, we cannot forget that the Middle Eastern setting of the Bible assumes that strangers are always potential enemies and hospitality was one means of adumbrating fear and making peace. If this had been remembered by many intellectuals of the eighteenth and nineteenth centuries, the entire course of theology might have been different. A number of factors made understanding strangers difficult because, in the minds of some, simply understanding *persons and people* had become problematic in the first place. The scientific discoveries of Alexander von Humboldt and Charles Darwin, the persistence of nationalism and colonial expansion, and Protestant and Catholic theologies of mission all contributed to this confusion. By then anatomists, anthropologists, and philologists (to name only a few specialists) had measured skull sizes (Johann Blumenbach), charted skin pigmentation (Immanuel Kant), and graded hair texture (Ernst Haeckel) in an effort to categorize human beings into types. A general suspicion of anyone unlike "me" became intertwined with the physical and social sciences so that "others," not just strangers, were regarded with amusement, fear, dread, and indifference.[1]

A portion of late-nineteenth-century Christian theology followed a similar path. For example, Isaac Dorner, who taught at universities all across Germany until his death in 1884, used the old Hippocratic schema of temperaments—phlegmatic, choleric, melancholic, and sanguine—as a key part of his system of ethics. For Dorner, the temperaments are marks not only of individuals but also of races and nations. He writes:

> The actual origin of the races may then be conceived in the following way: The four possible types of habitual fundamental mood into which the life of individuals can pass, are germinally involved in human nature itself. What the fundamental mood or temperament of the descendants shall be is especially dependent upon the constitution and mood of the parents at the time when they become parents. As, now, this fundamental mood may have been more and more widely transmitted, so these differences, if the descendants of like kind sought and found an outward nature in affinity with them, may, in the course of hundreds and thousands of years, by geographical and climactic conditions, by men's associating predominately with those of their own sort, and finally, by the operation of abnormal influences, have been developed and confirmed to the degree which the most marked races now existing present. Thus viewed, the races would be, as it were, temperaments or fundamental moods of human nature, fixed, though manifesting themselves in most manifold degrees, and to some extent in combinations.[2]

Dorner's typology favors the English to which "no one ascribes deficiency in sharply-defined traits" and denigrates the African who shows "plasticity, susceptibility for culture and for Christianity."[3] Although he does say that "Christian ethics, especially in our day, must admonish against an exaggeration of the value of nationality, and of a patriotism founded upon it"[4] he still holds that "the difference of races has doubtless not come to its present extreme without the influence of sin, and would be, under normal development, more nearly the same macrocosmically that brothers and sisters in the family circle are microcosmically." [5]

The heritage of the nineteenth century is still with us. Today, we often speak of "types of sinners," of "natural alliances," of "our kind of people," and of "national interest." These phrases indicate that we struggle to not only know who others are, but what *kind* of others they are. The phrases indicate that we live in a world of increasing classification and limited responsibilities. They indicate that the possibility of establishing our common humanity is eroding, that we have increased the number of people we perceive as enemies. Consider these words by Ann Coulter as she complained about the inconvenience of new airport security measures in the wake of the 9/11 tragedy:

> It is preposterous to assume every passenger is a potential crazed homicidal maniac. We know who the homicidal maniacs are. They are the ones cheering and dancing right now. We should invade their countries, kill their leaders and convert them to Christianity.[6]

It can only be imagined, though it would not take long to actually find out, the response her remarks brought forth in the Moslem world. At a minimum it would have been understood as a festered reminder of the Crusades, the issue that provokes more derision among the critics of Christianity than any other. Christians marching to war against Moslems under the banner of the cross is entirely antithetical to Jesus' command to love the enemy. Some scholars such as Thomas Madden have attempted to reframe the issue by arguing that the Crusades were largely defensive maneuvers against a relentless invader; that Crusaders did not slaughter masses of innocents but fought according to the principles of war that prevailed at the time; and, finally, that the intentions of the Crusaders were justified—even honorable.[7] Perhaps his interpretation of the Crusades will gain acceptance in time, but even if he is correct this would never make acceptable a theology of mission that is aligned with conversion by the sword.[8] All governments, even the most democratic, compassionate, and benevolent, rule by force. Thus, theologies of mission have to stand outside of the political sphere because the gospel is fundamentally a critique of the world and not in cooperation with it. When it happens, as in times like ours in which enemies seek to harm us, whatever political choices we make have to be done in the light of the fact that the gospel indicts all people as enemies of God. The greatest of care needs to be taken when using the terms *nonbeliever* and *enemy* lest Christianity be invalid from the start. The heart of believing in the gospel is the affirmation that Christians were once both strangers and enemies to God and who now have been brought into relationship with God through an act of divine hospitality. This is what Coulter's view seems to ignore.

Perhaps no modern theologian sought harder to avoid this error than Karl Barth. As he puts it, we must acknowledge that we are "crooked even in the knowledge of [our] crookedness"[9] and refuse to judge evil and sin by any standard other than that of Jesus Christ.[10] We must look into the mirror of Jesus Christ and "see ourselves as those who commit sin and are sinners."[11] The norm for establishing sin, the norm by which all are considered enemies of God, is the norm established by Jesus Christ in his death for us.

Barth's theology of reconciliation prevents adopting a viewpoint that distinguishes between types of God's enemies, strangers, and people. God has already judged all; Christ has been judged for all. Although those we consider enemies have done many disagreeable and even injurious things to us, and those who are strangers might do the same, we must concede that God has already gone before us and shown us divine hospitality. The more clearly I see myself having been once an enemy of God, a stranger to God, as having been once far from God, the more I see my reason for being hospitable toward others. As Barth writes:

> Jesus Christ fought his enemies, the enemies of God—as we all are (Rom. 5:10, Col. 1:21)—no, He loved His enemies, by identifying Himself with them. Compared with that what is the bit of forbearance or patience or humour or readiness to help or even interces-

sion that we are willing and ready to bring and offer in the way of loving our enemies?[12]

The Near and Distant Neighbor

It is clear that Barth believes that God's act of reconciliation toward us should forever change our behavior toward others. But do we have recourse to language that both recognizes our natural differences from one another yet still admits our mutuality? Barth suggests that there is and the term he uses for it is "near and distant neighbors." It is a remarkable phrase and it needs to be a critical part of theological hospitality and the doctrine of reconciliation.

The derivation of the phrase is in the second chapter of the Letter to the Ephesians. Typically, theological interest in this chapter is centered on whether being "by nature children of wrath" (Ephesians 2:3) establishes the doctrine of original sin *or* whether the true significance of the passage is about individual responsibility for sin. In my view, the exegetical debate should not distract us from seeing that the emphasis is upon the fact that God has reconciled both Jews and Gentiles through the cross of Jesus Christ. The passage does so by relying upon a full range of terms related to hospitality: aliens, strangers, citizenship, household members, and dwelling place (Ephesians 2:11-21). Given Barth's abiding interest in using biblical phrases to make theological points, it seems likely to me that he drew the term "near and distant neighbors" from verse 17, "So he [Jesus] came and proclaimed peace to you who were far off and peace to those who were near."

Barth does not use the actual term "near and distant neighbors" until the publication of *Church Dogmatics* III/4, at a point in which he is well into his lifelong project, but the concept is found as early as his lectures at Münster and Bonn between 1928 and 1931.[13] In the lectures "The Command of God the Creator," Barth divides the material into four sections: the command of life, calling, order, and faith. In the section on calling, Barth says that he must deal with "some of the narrower and broader circles within which life is lived," one of which is kinship.[14] In the paragraphs on kinship, Barth defines kinship as

[the] phenomenon that underlies the family as such, namely, that all of us stand in a special, if much graded, proximity to certain people; that they have the same ancestors and to that extent the same blood, that even if we do not all have a common present we share in part a common past, and that in the history of our ancestors we have, at any rate, a common prehistory.[15]

Kinship points beyond itself to larger circles of relationship that include clan, people, and nation. Barth goes on to argue that each of these only *appear* "to refer us to a close circle of fellowmen to the exclusion of all the rest."[16] The reality is that all peoples are members of the human family and this does away with artificial, rationalistic excuses that would be used to justify excluding anyone from our circle of care. He writes:

Even the deepest loyalty to kin and people cannot close our eyes to the fact that both these inner circles are enclosed by an even wider circle of blood relationship in which we stand by virtue of our calling by creation, which also claims our loyalty, and by which our conduct is also measured. Behind the relative is the fellow countryman and behind the fellow countryman is "the stranger that is within thy gates," and it is precisely the last of these who tells us, if we have not heard it before, that the true concern even in blood relationship is *humanity.*[17]

We should note the following. First, Barth uses the phrase "inner and wider circles" to describe the relationships between a person's family, neighbors, and nation. The fact of a common creation by God establishes this. Second, although we can see the common humanity of our family, neighbors, and nation on the basis of blood and race, it is ultimately the stranger that shows us who we actually are. The stranger is not just an abstract idea; our conduct toward the stranger is the measure of our obedience to the command of God.

This material from the Münster and Bonn lectures is carried over into *Church Dogmatics* where Barth takes up the question of how many "spheres" of relationship exist for each of us. Clearly there are the natural spheres of "man and woman" and "parent and child," but are there more? And if so, what are my obligations to those relationships? Here is where the idea of "near and distant" comes into play. He writes:

> The question faces us whether similarly a third and perhaps even a fourth sphere of such natural creaturely relationships does not claim our attention and perhaps find in the command of God confirmation of the fact that it, too, is essential to every man. Is there no more to say of man in his fellow-humanity than that he is man or woman, man and woman . . . ? Can we stay at the point which we have just reached, the relationship of parents and children and the wider family relationships involved? Is this really the limit of our enquiry? . . . is there not self-evidently suggested the concept of a greater nexus which is grounded in nature and fashioned in history and to which every man belongs and is bound . . . ? And if this is incontestable, does he not stand in a relationship which, like that of man and woman and parents and children, as an outer circle enclosing the inner, is an object of the divine command and is confirmed by it as essential to every man? We describe those to whom man seems to stand in this wider relationship as his near neighbours. . . . Those with whom he seems to stand in this widest relationship we call his distant neighbours.[18]

Barth's questions raise others. If I do stand in a natural relationship to others, do I have obligations toward them as well? Do I have spheres of responsibility that begin with those closest to me (my family, for example) and then widen in circumference so that I have different obligations to my next-door neighbor than I do to someone whom I do not know at all?

In theology that was roughly contemporary with Barth, these questions were not unusual, although the answers varied. One of the better answers is by Dietrich Bonhoeffer, who is critical of an idea of vocation that limits one's responsibility to simply those who are closest. Instead, he argues that vocation is the response of a person who has heard the call to live in fellowship with Jesus Christ. A true vocation means living responsibly by taking up a position against the world *in* the world. It is the place where one lives, works, and exists in relationship with others.

Thus, calling is not simply fulfilling one's duty as a citizen or an employee, nor is it found in a retreat from the world as the monastic life suggests. By being against the world while being in the world, calling is fulfilled in service to the neighbor. Bonhoeffer finds agreement with Friedrich Nietzsche's attack in *Thus Spoke Zarathustra* on legalistic interpretations of the neighbor. Nietzsche says:

> You are assiduous in your attentions to your neighbour and you find beautiful words to describe your assiduity. But I tell you that your love for your neighbour is a worthless love for yourselves. You go to your neighbour to seek refuge from yourselves and then you try to make a virtue of it; but I see through your "unselfishness" . . . Do I advise you to love your neighbour? I advise you . . . to love whoever is furthest from you!"[19]

Bonhoeffer's comment is:

> If beyond his neighbour a man does not know this one who is furthest from him, and if he does not know this one who is furthest from him as this neighbour, then he does not serve his neighbour but himself; he takes refuge from the free open space of responsibility in the comforting confinement of the fulfillment of duty. This means that the commandment of love for our neighbour also does not imply a law which restricts our responsibility solely to our neighbor in terms of space, to the man whom I encounter socially, professionally or in my family. My neighbour may well be one who is extremely remote from me, and one who is extremely remote from me may well be my neighbour.[20]

Bonhoeffer (through Nietzsche) is very persuasive. His point of view encourages us to be engaged with those farthest from us by seeing that we are called to serve. Yet, Barth's contribution helps us even more. Barth makes sure that we understand that fellowship with the stranger is not done in view of where the stranger *lives* but on the basis of what the stranger *is* for us. He correctly points out that the stranger helps us understand ourselves by showing us our common humanity. How does this occur? The answer lies in Barth's imaginative use of the image of concentric circles to represent the reality of human coexistence.

The circumference of any circle acts as a border that both includes and excludes. The border limits the number of objects, ideas, or in this case, people, that are part of a common set. Is it permissible in theology for us to speak of a circle whose borders are so fixed that it effectively constrains membership in another wider and concentric circle of humanity? Barth refutes this through an analysis of language, geography, and history. We should not believe that *language* represents an ultimate border, because we already know that dialects and regionalisms show our commonality in the midst of difference. We should not suppose that *geography* makes strangers, because geography only indicates a spatial relationship between peoples. There is nothing in the ground or soil from which we can abstract an independent theology or ethics of place, home, and motherland.[21] Nor can we say that any people have had such a pure and uninterrupted *history* that allows them to posit that they are somehow really different from others. Barth has the racial policies of Germany's recent past in mind when he writes:

> To-day, of course, there is no people—not even in Asia and Africa, let alone Europe and America—which can boast that its present members derive from the same families or clans and therefore constitute a unity of blood and race. It is impossible in practice to trace back the historical differences of peoples to natural causes, for in practice the majority of peoples have for centuries been physical mongrels, sometimes within the great types, sometimes cutting right across them. In most cases the different peoples derive from very different divisions and unions involving the strangest and most diverse physical mixtures. None of us has pure blood in any strict sense, nor does it seem helpful or necessary to have it.[22]

DYNAMIC CIRCLES OF RELATIONSHIPS IN THE LIGHT OF RECONCILIATION

This evidence destroys the idea that circles of relationship have boundaries that are so fixed as to limit our obligations toward others. Yet, Barth does not stop here. He constructs a positive case by arguing that the borders are essentially organic and dynamic. He believes that the borders between people are not fixed but porous, and his argument is based on four points. First, the relationship between near and distant neighbors is *reversible*. He writes, "One who is distant from one standpoint is near from another." Second, the relationship between near and distant neighbors is *fluid*. Where really does the boundary between peoples exist? Like the Alsace, the German-speaking region of France, language and geography can mean nothing when peoples are placed in proximity to one another. Third, the relationship between near and distant neighbors is *removable*. Nations are transitory; they come and go. All great names, peoples, or empires are lost eventually. Last, the relationship between near and distant neighbors is neither *original nor final*. As they have never been permanent in the past, so they will never be permanent in the future.[23]

There are at least two examples in *Church Dogmatics* that show how Barth applied his concept of near and distant neighbors and that underscore his commitment to viewing the neighbor, the stranger, or the enemy as persons who share with us a common humanity. The first example comes from the world of politics; the second, cultural history.

BEING BEHIND AND IN FRONT OF THE IRON CURTAIN

As a person forced to repatriate to Switzerland from Germany in 1933 because of his opposition to Nazism, Barth was familiar with the tyranny of borders and the powers that enforce them. This became apparent in a new way when, in 1948, he visited Hungary, one of the countries then under Soviet control.[24] His visit came two years after Winston Churchill had introduced the term "iron curtain" into the international vocabulary.[25] The term was reflective of the situation facing the flood of refugees and exiles that had or wanted to leave East for West, the new set of borders that were inked onto old maps, and the atmosphere of distrust among those who lived in the villages and cities on both sides of the postwar lines. Barth's addresses, letters, and conversations during and after his visit show the reality of this new metaphor. In one case, he explained in this way the situation that America, Russia, and the smaller nations of central Europe faced:

> Then between these safety-zones we have the famous Iron Curtain, through whose openings each of these two great powers proclaims its dislike of the other in abusive language and hurtful pin-pricks. Both are very fond of phrases like "the free community of the nations" and "peace." It is not very clear what either of them means by "freedom," but for the present there is no reason to suppose that either of them is seeking war, and to that extent is in fact seeking peace. What they have in common is, finally, this: that they are both afraid of the other, because they both feel encircled and threatened by the other.[26]

The iron curtain is a symbol of the deep roots of human sin that will eventually be taken away. In speaking to it Barth seeks to affirm that those in Hungary will see the time when they will not "be strangers and fugitives"; in the new world created by God, "they will be at home, they will be in their native land."[27] As for the cause of the situation, Barth marched a parade of criticisms against both communists and anticommunists, taking care to pin his disagreement with the current political status on the emptiness of Western civilization and the failure of the church to recognize its own complicity in the erection of the new realities.[28]

Barth picks up the theme of the iron curtain again in *Church Dogmatics* III/4 when the Soviet Union's increased control over vast portions of Eastern Europe signified a new understanding of strangers, allies, enemies, and neighbors. What theological response should one have to this? Barth gives his answer:

> There may for a time be iron curtains. But that is all. And no such curtain has ever proved to be impenetrable or fixed. Indeed, it is the function of a curtain not only to fall but also to rise again. This being the case, we must not confuse the contrast of near and distant neighbours with the creation of God and its immutable orders.[29]

All humanly constructed walls are provisional and temporary. In the best cases they are reminders of our responsibilities; they should not become barricades for our fears. God remains constant, not the changes wrought by human affairs. If we understand this, then we see that one way Barth interprets the stranger is by saying that a stranger is a person who witnesses to our common humanity in spite of any current arrangement of human affairs. What Barth encourages in his writings during this period is what he experienced during his visits. As he had been received and welcomed by the struggling churches in Hungary, he wanted them to be welcomed and understood by others.

Being among and with and as the Wandering Jews

The German idea of *wanderlust* speaks approvingly of those who wander in pursuit of the Romantic tradition: Johann Goethe, Friedrich von Schiller, and other writers of the early nineteenth century captured the joy of casual, independent travel. Others might perceive those in this tradition as strangers but not necessarily as "strange." [30] But tolerance for wanderlust was extended only to young men of a certain age and class who were seeking either to "find themselves" or to receive training in a vocation. All the rest were considered rootless, and because of that, threatening to the stability of society. For example, the Gypsies were considered itinerants, wanderers, stateless folk who, as they moved from place to place, found that they were perceived as magicians, beggars, and collaborators in the death of Christ and thereby subject to persecution. [31]

For many Europeans, Jews were considered threatening because they appeared to wander continuously and they stayed where they were not welcome. [32] Barth picks up this idea and begins by tracing the apparent "rootlessness" of the Jews to the fall of Jerusalem in AD 70. From that time forward their identity became rather ambiguous because they did not have a land of their own. This has, according to Barth (using the play on words found in the Old Testament prophet Hosea's description of Israel), made the Jews to be a people that are "not a people." He writes:

It [Israel] necessarily continues to exist in this unique way, as a people which in the usual sense of the word is not a people. It necessarily has history which strictly speaking is non-historical; the history of a guest and alien and stranger and exception amongst the nations, with the eternal Jew, perhaps, as its legendary pattern.[33]

The importance of Barth's citation of the "eternal Jew" (der ewige Jude) is not readily apparent for the person who reads it only in translation and is not aware of European cultural history. "The Wandering Jew" is a popular folktale, dating to at least the seventh century, about a Jewish man who verbally scorns Christ with the words, "Walk faster!" when Christ has paused to rest while carrying the cross to Golgotha. Christ answers, "I will, but you will walk until I come again."[34] The legend shows up, with all the variations that folktales accrue along the way, in art, literature, songs, and drama. The protagonist is sometimes called Malthus, sometimes Ahasuerus. And whereas the "Wandering Jew" tale could be romanticized, with the figure cast as noble, courageous, or wistful, the heart of the folktale is etiological: it explains why the Jews were wanderers and are to be wanderers until Christ returns at the end of the world. This was God's punishment upon them for their rejection of Jesus as the Messiah.

The legend influenced many historic forms of anti-Semitism and became one of the cornerstones for *modern* anti-Semitism as well.[35] One graphic example of this is the Nazi propaganda film *Der ewige Jude* (*The Eternal Jew*, 1940), which was preceded by a 1937 Munich exhibit of Jewish "degenerate art" and advertised as *The Eternal Jew*.[36] Produced under Joseph Goebbels and directed by Fritz Hippler, the film was shown across Germany and was required viewing for members of the SS.[37] The film depicts Polish Jews as morally bankrupt, dirty, lazy, ugly, conniving, and disease-bearing rats. The film argued that there was an international Jewish conspiracy infecting every segment of society:

Comparable with the Jewish wanderings through history are the mass migrations of an equally restless animal, the rat. . . . Wherever rats appear they bring ruin, they ravage human property and foodstuffs. In this way they spread disease: plague, leprosy, typhoid, cholera, dysentery, etc. They are cunning, cowardly, and cruel, and are found mostly in packs. In the animal world they represent the element of craftiness and subterranean destruction—no different from the Jews among mankind! [38]

Against this background Barth argues that although Jews are a wandering people, their wandering is a sign of God's providence, not God's punishment. Stripped of land, language, and history, they are preserved, accompanied, and ruled by God. Even to this moment they are a testament to God's faithfulness to the covenant of election. The continued existence of the Jews is not an accident or a miracle but is a sign of God's faithfulness and grace, of the constancy of God's will and decree. Barth sees in the wanderings of the Jews a forceful subversion of any anti-Semitic ideology that would brand the Jews as "no people" when they are the "people of God." [39] Jews belong to God even after their rejection of the Messiah. They remain the elected people who belong to God even in their state of unfaithfulness to their election. They have "traversed world history" as "the human servant[s] of God"; "as bearers of light and salvation." [40] One section of his argument is particularly moving:

Living only by the grace of God, he is not allowed anything of his own by which to justify or adorn himself, or to vindicate himself and make his own way in world history as a whole. All that he can do is simply to be there. He cannot be overlooked, or banished, or destroyed—for the grace of God holds and upholds him—but he is not allowed the glory which counts in world history generally. He is everywhere the minority. He is everywhere the guest and stranger. He is always the one who has no home, no city, no temple. How can he have, when the judgment of God is necessarily active and revealed in him together with the grace of God? Abraham was a stranger in the land of promise. Moses was a stranger to his own people. So were the prophets. The foxes have holes, and the birds of the air have nests, but the Son of Man hath no where to lay His head. The elect of God, whose very existence proclaims light and salvation to the world, but in whom the judgment of all flesh is also active and revealed, will always and necessarily be strangers in the world, with no home of their own. In this sense, too, the Jews are the elect of God.[41]

As the elect of God of have rejected the Messiah, the Jew reveals, as a mirror, the truth about all people, Christian or not, or whether we speak of ourselves as individuals or as a group. The mirror reveals a self that is prideful, self-righteous, and in opposition to God.[42] The metaphor of the mirror describes all humanity in their rebellion against God. None of humanity likes to acknowledge that God's mercy is the "sole and mighty basis of human existence."[43] But as the Jews have been preserved in their wandering by God's grace, so too has all of humanity been reconciled by God's grace. This realization only comes when one first acknowledges "that no one, neither people nor individual, really has a home in world history, that no one is finally secure, that we are all pushed about, that we are all eternal strangers, since it is only in God that we are finally at home and secure."[44] We need the grace and mercy of God in the face of life's brevity and passing.

HOSPITALITY AND RECONCILIATION

What has Barth taught us? How does understanding hospitality in relationship to reconciliation help us? Although it is important to give priority first and foremost to divine love, it seems entirely unlikely to me that anything short of the admission that all people are aliens and strangers to God will ever be able to bring about the reconciliation with one another that our world needs. Barth outlines four principles that should guide our encounters with others. First, we must "look the other in the eye."[45] We should see others (neighbors, enemies, and strangers) in such a way that they are visible to us not as a mere object but as a reflection of our own fallen and redeemed humanity. Seeing is inhuman if it is not the seeing of another human. Barth writes:

It is a great and solemn and incomparable moment when two men look themselves in the eye and discover one another. This moment, this mutual look, is in some sense the root-formation of all human-ity without which the rest is impossible. But it is to be noted again that in the strict sense it can take place only in duality, as I and Thou look one another in the eye. Where a man thinks he sees and knows a group, or a group a man, or one group another group, ambiguity always arises.[46]

Second, to encounter another is to engage in hearing. Whereas seeing another human is critical, it is only in speaking and hearing that one crosses into the boundary of relationship. The real prob-lem with encountering a stranger is our imagination: it is why we begin each new encounter with the question, Who are you? Hospitality requires being open to the self-declaration of others, allowing them to say who they are. It is in this way that my uncer-tainty about who the other is is removed. Until this occurs I am captive to the possibility that what I have seen is incomplete.[47]

Third, being in encounter is the rendering of mutual aid. Being human consists of living with and for one another. Only by active standing by the side of others is my own humanity complete. We are made for community. "My humanity," Barth writes, "depends upon the fact that I am always aware, and my action is deter-mined by the awareness, that I need the assistance of others as a fish needs water."[48] Finally, being in encounter takes the form of seriousness when seeing, hearing, and assisting is done with gladness.[49] This gladness takes us to the heart of Christian hospital-ity: I see the stranger, even the armed and threatening enemy, and because I know that Christ has died and been raised for both of us, the final and ultimate seriousness of their threat is taken away.

As chilling as it may be to imagine, I can understand if there are children somewhere who play a game called "World Trade Center Bombers." Why not? The game has it all: jet planes, tall buildings to crash, fire, noise, and destruction. All you have to do is fly around with your arms outspread, weave erratically, and then plunge straight ahead. The bigger noise you make on impact the more accolades you can expect.

I can think this way because when I was younger my brother and I played a game called "Russians versus Americans at the

Olympics." The games themselves were fairly simple: the picnic-table vault, the lawn-chair hurdle, and the tree/fence/patio race. Because we were Americans, we were bound by the rules of fair play: the Russians had to win a share of the events. But in the end, when the gold was actually on the line, we pulled out all the stops for Old Glory. As I think about it now, there was something more than simple competition going on inside our tightly laced high-top sneakers. The implications were geopolitical. We were Americans; the Russians were enemies. There is not much room to believe that my brother and I were unique. Viewing Russian athletes as antiheroes was standard fare in popular sports reporting.[50] However, we lived in a military town, with real nuclear weapons and with real radars that regularly spun around looking for incoming warheads. This happened so often that it was actually disappointing to walk by and not see the radars turning. Because of this I have to judge that the games we played reflected a sense of the world that was a little more acute than that of children who just stuck with cops and robbers.

Still, I am bothered by this question: why don't children play a game called "International Peacekeepers"? Why don't they play "Truth and Reconciliation Commission"? Why isn't there a game called "Doctors Without Borders"? Am I naive? Is it simply that such games are too high-minded for children, that children are naturally competitive, that their sense of the world has more room for contrast than for ambiguity? Perhaps we have failed to guide them. Perhaps we have lived with so many walls, with so many borders, with so many types of strangers and enemies that we have led them to believe that you can live in a neighborhood but you cannot create one. If so, we are the worst of sinners.

Chapter Three

"She Laid It on Us"

GUESTS AND HOSTS IN FEMINIST
PERSPECTIVE

Hospitality requires both guests and hosts and cannot exist without the two working together: one offers, the other receives. The offer and acceptance of hospitality can take place anywhere there is space to share and the authority to share it. Yet the household is the *essential* sphere for hospitality: it is the place where host and guest meet in a way that is not duplicated in other forums. When we say, "Come to *my* house," we are saying something fundamentally different from when we invite someone into *our* country, into *our* town, or into *our* neighborhood. Although those settings, or circles, invite the stranger to know us in ever-narrowing and more intimate ways, the intimacy of my home can never be usurped. This perspective suggests that the New Testament's emphasis on the home, on the household, is of seminal significance for understanding the third foundation of theological hospitality.

During the time of the emerging New Testament church, hospitality put women at the center of theological discourse and conflict. In commenting on 1 Timothy 5:10, where showing hospitality is required for a widow if she is to receive the financial support of the church, Carolyn Osiek and David L. Balch say:

41

This simple line gives us a glimpse of the role of women as providers of services in the church, especially widows with room in their houses. They were the ones best prepared to receive visiting missionaries, teachers, and other Christian travelers. They too along with their households may have been drawn into the theological conflicts that were beginning to surface at this time.[1]

Osiek and Balch are too modest. Given the fact that the emerging church met exclusively in houses—except for the brief period of time when they still associated with the temple (Acts 2:46; 3:1)—there was no other forum for theological debates to be handled. We are speaking of the pre-Constantinian church; the church before councils, basilicas, magisterial bishops; the church that met in the houses of Chloe and Priscilla and Nympha. To say that women *may* have been drawn in does not give full weight to the way in which hospitality and the experience of women met together to produce one of the most radical movements ever to emerge in the Greco-Roman world. This movement was dependent upon women's notions of space and authority.

The long-standing social, cultural, political, and economic associations of women as hosts of households requires, indeed necessitates, that their reflections, particularly those of feminist theologians, on the use of space and authority should be considered in the construction of a theology of hospitality for today.[2] A close look at the conversion of Lydia in Acts 16 in the light of feminist theological reflections on space and authority will bring about a better understanding of the theological dynamics of hosting.

SHE LAID IT ON US: LYDIA AS HOST, PAUL AS GUEST

Commentators on the book of Acts tend to view the conversion of Lydia as part of Paul's expanding journey into the Gentile world. There is no doubt that the figure of Paul dominates the book of Acts. Yet reading the book with only Paul in mind does not do justice to Luke's narrative of the emerging church and of the dozens of people whose story is told along the way. Acts presents a series of rather dramatic stories about public preaching and conversion but the actual day-to-day spread of Christianity was far more mundane and practical: it went from "house to house" (Luke 5:42; 10:7; Acts 20:20). The New Testament letters explain that many of these churches met in the houses of women: Chloe in 1 Corinthians 1:11; Priscilla in 1 Corinthians 16:19 and Romans 16:5; and Nympha in Colossians 4:15. Among the women who had a church meeting in her house was Lydia. When the narrative in Acts 16 is read in a way that does not marginalize her, which makes the narrative less about Paul and more about Lydia, it becomes apparent that she was among the greatest contributors to the emerging understanding of theological hospitality in the early church.

Elisabeth Schüssler Fiorenza's general argument against traditional exegesis and methods bears directly on our reading of the story of Lydia and Paul:

> Women's leadership and contributions to early Christianity can only become historically viable when we abandon our outdated patriarchal-androcentric model of early Christian beginnings. Even when the New Testament source texts suggest a different meaning, such androcentric models can understand early Christian women only as marginal figures or see them in subordinate "feminine" roles which are derived from our own contemporary experience and understandings of reality.[3]

In order to understand Lydia's contribution, we must return to the narrative with fresh eyes. The verses are among the most subtle, but also the most important, in the New Testament for understanding hospitality. The most important insight will come from comprehending her insistence that Paul and his fellow travelers stay at her house. The passage reads:

> On the Sabbath day we went outside the gate by the river, where we supposed there was a place of prayer; and we sat down and spoke to the women who had gathered there. A certain woman named Lydia, a worshiper of God, was listening to us; she was from the city of Thyatira and a dealer in purple cloth. The Lord

opened her heart to listen eagerly to what was said by Paul. When she and her household were baptized, she urged us saying, "If you have judged me to be faithful to the Lord, come and stay at my home." And she prevailed upon us. (Acts 16:13-15)

Luke reports that Lydia's first offer of hospitality to Paul and company was denied. In the face of this she repeated her offer in stronger terms. In this instance, Luke says, "She prevailed upon us." The Greek word for prevail is *parabiazesthai*, a word that originally meant "to force" or "to exercise violence" (Matthew 12:12; Luke 16:16). Luke uses this term to describe the insistence of the two disciples in Emmaus that Jesus (as a stranger!) join them for dinner and rest (Luke 24:29). The Septuagint uses the term to describe an effort to get someone to do something he is not inclined to do, sometimes actually shaming the person into doing what the speaker wants (2 Kings 2:17). In this case, Lydia's intention is not so much in shaming Paul, nor is she engaging in the conventions of Mediterranean hospitality in which a modest offer is met by a polite refusal followed by a second escalated and more vigorous request. The sense of what Lydia did to Paul's group was that "she laid it on us."[4] The significance of what she did was to call Paul to account for the meaning of *his* gospel and *her* baptism. In Lydia's reckoning, one side of the equation was in danger of being slighted.

Lydia met Paul, the young disciple Timothy, Luke, and Silas "some days" after they arrived in Philippi (Acts 16:11). This is one of the larger traveling groups depicted in Acts.[5] Upon reaching Philippi, they remain in the city for several days and talk to no one until "a woman from Thyatira" welcomes them. Lydia's gender and origin are important because they depart from the vision by Paul that instigated his travel to Macedonia in the first place. In that vision, Luke tells us that "there stood a man of Macedonia" who pleaded with Paul saying, "Come over to Macedonia and help us" (Acts 16:9). However, when they come to Philippi there is no *man* to greet them; Lydia, a woman, does.[6] Moreover, the men of the city had ample opportunity to welcome them because they had been in the city for three days. Paul and company were homeless strangers in a city where they were not even noticed by the men, let alone greeted, welcomed, and received. The stress of the passage seems to be that the travelers were in sad shape. This was not the case in other cities.

Just like travelers of today, the practice of writing to friends for housing was common in the ancient world.[7] Priscilla and Aquila arrange housing for Apollos as he leaves them in Alexandria and sails to Achaia (Acts 18:27). As his letter to Philemon shows, Paul would ask for housing even when he had differences of opinion with a potential host (Philemon 22). When Paul sends his letter to the Romans, the letter carrier is Phoebe, a deacon of the church at Cenchreae; he expects that the Romans will welcome her, a request that calls to mind his plea within the letter to "contribute to the needs of the saints; extend hospitality to strangers" (Romans 12:13). In fact, the use of the Greek word *propempo*,[8] sometimes translated as "to speed on the way," indicates that technical and standardized language for hospitality was emerging in the social network of the early church.[9] However, writing letters to Philippi was pointless since this was an unevangelized city and there were no believers to ask. Where would they have stayed?

In the absence of someone waiting to receive them they would have had five choices: lodging at an inn, sleeping in the streets, pitching a tent, renting private housing, or asking for a guest room at the synagogue. Christians avoided the inns because of their association with magical practices and immorality.[10] Inns were not comfortable, either. Everett Ferguson writes:

> The wine was often adulterated (or after the patron was drunk on good wine, bad was substituted), sleeping quarters were filthy and insect and rodent infested, inn-keepers were extortionate, thieves were in wait, government spies were listening, and many were nothing more than brothels.[11]

Sleeping in the streets meant exposure to wild dogs (1 Kings 14:11; Psalm 59:6; Revelation 22:15). As for sleeping in his tent, we have to surmise that Paul used tents in his travels on the road between cities, but we have no direct evidence of his using a tent once he came to a city. Renting was an option and Luke notes that Paul rented a private home in Rome, but this was because of the exceptional circumstances of his arrest and is not indicative of his normal practice (Acts 28:16, 30).

This leaves staying at the synagogue. Typically, when Paul arrived in a new city he made his way straight to the synagogue (Acts 9:20; 13:5, 14; 14:1; 17:1, 10). Synagogues were scattered across ancient urban areas: Rome had at least eleven and they catered to distinct social groups. Like "the synagogue of the Freedmen" in Acts 6:9, synagogues were differentiated by language, social standing, organization, and other factors.[12] Synagogues were not merely places of worship: they were community-oriented places, fit out with benches, where people ate meals together, observed Sabbaths and festivals, organized the collection of the temple tax dues, taught their children, arranged for the transmission of the first-fruits, and heard civil law cases.[13] They could pride themselves on their hospitality. The inscription on the Ophel synagogue, dated from around the first century AD, states:

> Theodotos, son of Vettenos, priest and archisynagogos, son of an archisynagogos, grandson of an archisynagogos, built the synagogue for the reading of the Law and for instruction in the commandments. (He built) also the guest house, the rooms, and the water facility as a lodging for travelers in need. Of this synagogue his fathers, the elders, and Simonides laid the foundations.[14]

There is no indication that Paul ever stayed *in* a synagogue in the cities he visited but there are indications that *through* the synagogues Paul made connections that could have afforded him housing. This occurs in Acts 18:7 where Paul stays with Titius Justus, whose house was "next door to the synagogue." In Acts 18:20 when members of the synagogue in Ephesus receive Paul favorably, they ask him "to stay longer," and we may presume that they arranged for his housing.

But was there a synagogue in Philippi? Paul goes to what Luke calls "a place of prayer" (*proseuchai*) that may or may not have been a synagogue. A place of prayer could be either a physical building or simply a topological description of an area used by some for prayer, in this case a place near the river.[15] When he arrives there he comes across a gathering *(sunerchesthai)* of women. It is important to realize that the women were not just milling about but had come to the place of prayer by the river to engage in a deliberate, purposeful event that implies community, as Luke's usage demonstrates when he describes the shared work of mission and discipleship of the women who had followed the body of Jesus to its grave (Luke 23:55).[16] Paul's usage underscores the idea of purposefulness: he uses the word to speak of what the Corinthians do when they come together as a church (1 Corinthians 14:26; cf. 11:18, 20, 33-34), or of the sexual union of husband and wife (1 Corinthians 7:5). What needs to be seen is that Paul (as was his custom) intends to preach and teach in Philippi exactly as he does in other places. At the same time, Lydia and the women with her are doing exactly what their custom was as well! This was *their* place of prayer. They are the hosts of an established religious community that Paul comes into as a stranger, and they receive him as a guest, according him the courtesy of teaching and preaching to them.

So, at her place of prayer, she has received this stranger. But what type of woman was Lydia? First, she was not "European." Frank Stagg writes:

> Modern ideas of "Asia" and "Europe" are foreign to the situation in Acts. The Roman provinces of Asia, Macedonia, and Achaia constituted a great Greco-Roman cultural center on the shores of the Aegean Sea. They were not divided into "Asia" and "Europe" or into "East" and "West." Rackham aptly states it in saying, "The Macedonian did not say, 'Come over into Europe,' but 'Come over into Macedonia.'" The divide between East and West was not the Bosporus or Dardanelles, but the Taurus mountains.[17]

Second, Lydia is "a worshiper of God" *(sebomene ton theon)*, the same as Titius, whom Paul took shelter with in Acts 18:7. Luke makes a note of pointing out that sometimes a *sebomene* was hostile to the message of Christianity (Acts 13:43, 50; 17:4, 17).

Third, Lydia's name is an *ethnicon*, a type of appellative given to slaves that describes origin, nationality, and racial or ethnic attributes in lieu of a personal name.[18] In this case it indicates that she was named for the city of Lydia in the region of Thyatira. Trades like Lydia's were primarily done by slaves, and freed slaves could only work in the same locale if their liberator would not suffer economic or social injury.[19] Thus, Lydia's migration to Philippi may have been compelled by legal and economic factors and not because she had the freedom to travel about peddling her goods as she pleased. What we need to notice, however, is that Lydia is, if not an immigrant, someone who is at the very least away from home and is living in Macedonia as an outsider. In Macedonia, it was not hard to rouse up suspicion of outsiders (cf. Acts 16:20). This, too, adds to the difficulties of her life.

Fourth, since workers in the same trade or of the same ethnic background and citizenship status lived near or with one another, Lydia's household might be fairly interpreted as a community of foreign women who shared the work of dying fabric, with Lydia serving as *patrona*.[20] The popular conception of Lydia as a wealthy woman who dealt in expensive fabrics is misleading. A more accurate rendering of *purpurie* is a person who works in the manufacturing and sale of dyed products.[21] Although dye houses were owner operated and often employed hired help, and both genders worked as dyers and dealers, textile production was still considered women's work and was thus looked down upon by the general public. Moreover, large-scale production of textiles was not common during this period, so Lydia's work was most likely a subsistence occupation for herself and her house.[22]

Dye houses had a terrible odor because the process of dying wool involved the use of large amounts of animal urine. So to counter the offensive nature of this work, dye houses were located outside the city gates.[23] Moreover, like leather tanning, the dying of fabrics was done by hand, which caused a visible stigma. Working with dyes changes the appearance of the worker's body: the repeated dipping, washing, and stirring of fabrics in vats stains everything from the fingers to the middle forearms. Lydia was probably discolored, and her purplish skin was a constant reminder of her social position. A quotation from Plutarch is striking: "Often we take pleasure in a thing, but we despise the one who made it. Thus we value aromatic salves and purple clothing, but the dyers and salve-makers remain for us common and low craftspersons." [24]

Consequently, we can believe that Lydia was not a wealthy woman who enjoyed the prosperity that came from dealing in luxury goods, but was a freed slave who made her living in a profession marginalized by philosophers and the public alike. She was conscious of what living beyond the city gates as a migrant worker in a foreign land meant for her social and political status; she was a person open to new religious convictions and gathered around her a circle of women, some of whom lived and worshiped with her.

OPEN HEART, OPEN HOME

Lydia's open heart led Paul to a new understanding of place. By her persistent appeals, Lydia goes beyond the accepted tradition that a woman should only be host to those with whom she is familiar. Her reception of Paul opens her home to the public; a home that was once hidden becomes visible. Prior to her meeting Paul, Lydia's home was hidden from society and from view in the sense that her status as a God-fearer, a migrant, and a member of a despised trade contributed to her not being seen. To enter into her household was to enter a world of complete otherness and only someone who was willing to accept the marginalization of Lydia's existence could cross over.

Lydia's invitation to Paul is an invitation for him to experience topophilia—the affectionate response to a physical environment.[25] Tuan writes:

These [responses] differ greatly in intensity, subtlety, and mode of expression. The response to environment may be primarily aesthetic: it may then vary from the fleeting pleasure one gets from a view to the equally fleeting but far more intense sense of beauty that is suddenly revealed. The response may be tactile, a delight in the feel of air, water, and earth. More permanent and less easy to express are feelings that one has toward a place because it is home, the locus of memories.[26]

It is important to notice that whereas natural or geographical structures such as rock formations, lakes, or wooded glens are the obvious places where topophilia can occur, the concept does not exclude physical structures created by humans. Thus, a physical dwelling, whether it is a country lodge or a downtown loft, is a site that can evoke an emotional response. Topophilia has symbolic depth that allows a person to attribute sacredness to an ordinary place; it is the impulse behind giving places names, marking them with stones, and enhancing them with gardens.

We should remember that topophilia carries with it a notion of seeing, touching, smelling, and hearing that which we have not encountered before. A place becomes a site of topophilia when it is experienced as a moment of revelation that promises to be repeated. The instance may be momentary, but the memory and promise of it remain long after we have left. The experience of topophilia must be considered a key concept of hospitality.

This experience, however, would exclude all places in which harm is done. Topophilia is not present where there is pain, discomfort, oppression, or in environments known to produce distrust, loneliness, isolation, and suspicion. Curtaining, dividing, or fencing a place often has the effect of removing the possibility of topophilia. When a person is put out of a house or shut out of public or private spaces through curtaining, segregating, or fencing, topophilia has been excluded as well.

Because the feeling of topophilia can be so strong, because it is associated with housing, and because "women's places" have been in the home, reflections about topophilia show up in literature written by women. Zora Neale Hurston's *Their Eyes Were Watching God*, a work often cited by womanist theologians, gives two striking examples.[27]

In the novel, the protagonist is a young woman named Janie. Janie's first consciousness of herself as a woman and not as a child is when she sits under the pear tree and dreams of romantic love. What might be an ordinary tree to anyone else is for Janie a place of both being and becoming. Hurston emphasizes the extraordinariness of the little garden by saying that it was for Janie a place of revelation, a place of summoning, and a place of waiting. Here we have an example of topophilia (it is a place of memory and revelation) that is heavily suggestive of the Near Eastern concept of paradise. Hurston's own work as a cultural anthropologist, as well as a childhood spent in church, made her sensitive to the importance of Edenic and sacred places; so she stresses Janie's real desire to share both her feelings about the garden and the space itself. When she is forbidden from going there, Janie's soul and her memory of the garden wither.

A second striking example for understanding the interplay of topophilia and womanist discourse is Janie's conversation with her old friend Pheoby while they sit on Janie's back porch. Hurston begins and ends the novel with this single back-porch conversation. The opening and closing scenes reveal all the classic marks of hospitality: the exchange of welcome, the sharing of food, and the washing of feet. Then, when Janie has finished telling her story, she begins to disclose the meaning of it all. It contains a summation of the moral truth she has learned:

> Now, dat's how everything wuz, Pheoby, jus' lak Ah told yuh. So Ah'm back home agin and Ah'm satisfied tuh be heah. Ah done been tuh de horizon and back and now Ah kin set heah in mah house and live by comparisons. Dis house ain't so absent of things lak it used tuh be befo' Tea Cake come along. It's full uh thoughts, 'specially dat bedroom.[28]

Janie says that although she has traveled and journeyed far from home, it is this particular place that is richest for her. She has been to the horizon, the far limits of human experience, and has returned to her home, a place she loves—the place where the sun never sets on her memories. Even more importantly, Janie entrusts Pheoby with her story in a hospitable setting that brings with it certain ethical ideas: honesty, vulnerability, and respect.

The linking of topophilia with hospitality is expressed in a different way by N. Lynne Westfield when she explains a womanist notion of "concealed gatherings" in her theology of hospitality.[29] Westfield recounts how a gathering she participated in, the Dear Sisters Literary Group, met in one another's homes to read, share, and gather resilience. Resilience is important to her and she uses it to distinguish between herself and other womanist theologians who choose to stress the importance of such gatherings for survival. Resilience describes "a spiritual tenacity" that "connotes a more communal sense of being and belonging."[30] By this account, a womanist is a person who transforms an ordinary space into a place she loves and invites others to share in. To a passerby the house appears like every other house or apartment in the neighborhood. But for those to whom it has been revealed, the physical structure is the well of refreshment. A womanist aims not to merely *make a place* for hospitality, but looks to see how, as a host, her hospitality *makes a place*.

This Is My House, But These Are God's Rules

The ancient household was not democratic; nor was the ancient church. As the leader of her house, Lydia could do as she wished, and she would have had authority to admit or reject someone from her house. In fact, the New Testament indicates that patrons often acted presumptively, with disheartening results for the other congregants (3 John 10). On what basis did she invite Paul into her home? Was it on the basis of her status as a homeowner alone? I do not think so.

Conversion in the early church was an emotional experience. Paul's letters frequently refer to the wave of emotions that followed or preceded baptism.[31] In the context of Acts 16, the baptism of the Philippian jailer is surrounded by emotional language: he "trembles" before Paul and Silas (16:29); he shows repentance and compassion by washing their wounds (16:33); he rejoices that he has become a believer in God (16:34). Lydia's conversion is just as dramatic and had no less of an impact on her. It helps us understand her speech insisting that Paul come to her house.

Commentators frequently misunderstand Lydia's speech. For example, F. Scott Spencer argues that when Lydia says, "If you have judged me to be faithful to the Lord, come and stay at my home," the words she utters are suppliant rather than prophetic, thoroughly subject to Paul's authority.[32] Whereas Spencer is correct that Lydia's speech is short compared to the speeches made by others in the book of Acts, it is not correct to argue that she is deferring to Paul's authority; rather, she is challenging it by forcing him to recognize her status as a believer. Luise Schottroff blames Paul's resistance on his alleged misogyny and this, too, is wrong.

> Paul's refusal and that of his companions do not reflect the modesty of folk who are reluctant to accept hospitality; rather, they are the refusals of Christian men to grant women, whose baptism they have just authorized or performed, and those baptismal rights that concern their role as women. Lydia argued, implicitly or explicitly, on the basis of the Christian baptismal confession, which we know from Gal. 3:28; the Paul of Acts of the Apostles behaved similarly to the Paul of the *Acts of Thecla*: because you are a woman, you are seducible and a seductress and therefore dangerous as a hostess or a leader of the Christian community. Lydia offers hospitality, and consequently, political protection, but Paul refuses it because he regards women as untrustworthy (i.e., not to be "faithful" in the sense of v. 15), even though baptism has just sealed this faithfulness. Lydia addresses this contradiction and she prevails. The power to offer political resistance is manifested in this case by her offer of hospitality. But that power is undermined by the role of women in society. She has to fight for both together, which is what Paul does not grasp.[33]

Schottroff is wrong about Paul's view of women. Paul names an impressive array of women who were his coworkers, he insists that they be treated by others as full partners and afforded full respect, and he requires believers to attend assemblies of the church hosted by women (1 Corinthians 1:11; 16:19; Romans 16:5; Colossians 4:15). But Schottroff is right that as a Christian, Lydia's authority to host derives not from her home ownership but from her baptism. Her authority to greet, to receive, and to protect the stranger comes from her union with Christ (Romans 6:1-5). It is on the basis of her baptism that she challenges any cultural notion that her house is not "fitting" for visitors. Lydia upbraids Paul by requiring him to assess the meaning of the baptism he has just witnessed. She understands that Paul should understand.

The feminist theology of Letty Russell also helps us understand Lydia's hospitality. Russell has continually pressed home the idea that theology ought to spring from what she calls "table talk."[34] She noticed that the accidental reorganization of church furniture from its traditional setting of pews in horizontal lines to benches placed in a circle radically changed how members of her congregation related to one another. Power began to shift from the pulpit to the congregants as each member now experienced being part of a spiral of authority that moved from the edges toward the center. She convinced the elders to make this change permanent, and with it came an ecclesiology that could connect with those on the margins. Her writing on ecclesiology keeps this experience in mind as she develops the idea of "the round table principle." This principle is used in answering the question, "How do we develop a feminist theory about the church that makes sense of women's reality and experiences of oppression and yet continues to affirm Jesus Christ as the source of life and connection in the Christian community?"[35] According to Russell, the principle

> looks for ways that God reaches out to include all those whom society and religion have declared outsiders and invites them to gather around God's table of hospitality. The measure of the adequacy of the life of a church is how it is connected to those on the margin, whether those the NRSV calls "the least of these who are members of my family" are receiving the attention to their needs for justice and hope (Matt. 25:40).[36]

Russell's interest in the oppressed and the ignored is consonant with that of other liberation theologians. It is standard practice for liberation theologians such as Gustavo Gutiérrez to speak of doing theology from "below." But she prefers the language of margins rather than "above" and "below" because she feels that when liberation theologians use this language they are repeating the mistakes of traditional theology. The language of "above" and "below" reinforces notions of hierarchy. Instead, the margin empowers women to "move from margin to center so that their voices may be heard."[37]

But gaining a place to speak is not the end of the matter. For Russell theology is only sufficient when women's critical social analysis results in their "talking back" to the tradition. The phrase "talking back" is used by the feminist bell hooks to describe how women have been silenced and shamed by being told that they should be silent, submissive, and second.[38] Women, like children, are told by patriarchal individuals and systems, "Don't back talk me"; "Don't be uppity or sassy"; and "Don't forget your place." By naming this language and its actions, hooks is attempting to subvert the dominant culture. "Talking back" becomes a method of decentering and reconstructing the language of authority. Russell feels that by "talking back" to the tradition, women "[claim] a voice at the center of the church as interpreter of what it means to followers of Christ in contemporary society" and she agrees with hooks's claim that "it should be understood that the libratory voice will necessarily confront, disturb, demand that listeners even alter ways of hearing and learning."[39]

We have been probing the question of the host's authority. In what way does Russell help us construct a theology of the host? Clearly, Lydia's authority to be a host does not only derive from her being a householder. She does have a place to offer, and in the past that authority came from her being a business owner, an employer, and a person whose religious convictions had called her to gather around her a circle of women who shared her beliefs. However, as a Christian, Lydia's authority to host derives first from her baptism. Her authority to greet, to receive, and to protect the stranger is concomitant with her reception of the gospel of Jesus Christ, as demonstrated in her immersion and union with Christ (Romans 6:1-5). It is from this position that she "talks back" to any cultural notion that her house is not "fitting" for visitors, that her invitation is only the first round of a Middle Eastern negotiation in which demurring is *de rigueur,* or that her offer needs to be legitimated by Paul's authority. Lydia asserts her authority, as Christ has given it to her.

***

In this chapter I have illustrated how feminist theology illuminates the nature of the place where hospitality is offered and the source of a host's authority for that place. When Lydia's story is retold from the point of view of women on the margins of society, when it is retold from the point of view of Christian hospitality's willingness to open itself to outsiders, and when it is retold from the point of view that authority is not grounded in the availability of physical possessions but in being possessed by Christ, then we have come to see hosting from the perspective of feminist understandings of hospitality. Moreover, it opens the door to several advances in ecclesiology. First, it values the opportunity to share. Second, an ecclesiology like this values solidarity with the least that goes beyond mere acceptance to empowerment. Guests who leave this circle are refreshed and reminded of what they have experienced by the continuing gift of fellowship. Third, it is insistent and demanding; it breaks through the conventional and the comfortable by calling forth the real significance of baptism. It is a baptism that places one in the household of God and from which hospitality emerges.

Chapter Four

"Remember My Chains"

HOSPITALITY AND ESCHATOLOGY IN PRISON LIFE

I n the parable of the sheep and the goats, Jesus speaks for the sick, the naked, and the imprisoned—those whose voices either have become raspy and hoarse because of desperation or have been silenced by the indifference of others. The repeated refrain of the parable, "When did we see you?" could just as easily have been, "When did we hear you?"

The determination to speak and be heard in the midst of all circumstances, particularly by means of letters from prison, was one of the earliest practices in the Christian community. Amid their suffering the writers of prison letters gave greetings to past hosts, encouraged the reception of new guests, and were a means of planning for future visits both inside and outside of prison. From the confines of their cells the writers witnessed to the importance of hospitality. When Paul writes from prison to the Colossians, "I, Paul, write this greeting with my own hand. Remember my chains. Grace be with you" (4:18), he is using his letter to remain visible and audible, as all prisoners hope to be.

He had a hard way to go. Letters differ from spoken words because an orator can judge the emotional effect of a speech upon listeners right away, whereas the sender of a letter only experiences emotion at the time of the letter's writing, but not at the time of the letter's reception. Second, whereas orators never have complete certainty that they have been understood, letter writers not only do not have certainty that they have been understood but they also never have certainty that their letter has been read or even arrived.

Given the vagaries of prison life, the interplay between faith, hope, and time is more heightened for prisoners than for ordinary folk. In fact, time is, next to the concept of space, the critical element in understanding the metaphysics of prison life. Contemporary prisoners have developed their own language for this; they speak of "doing time," "serving time," "passing time," and "hard time." And then there is "Buck Rodgers Time," a parole date so far into the next century that a prisoner cannot imagine release.[1]

Christian prisoners fend off this despair by making use of three perspectives of time: the chronological, the ritualistic, and the imperatival. Paul's request that Timothy "come before winter" indicates an awareness of chronological time (2 Timothy 4:21). Paul adopts a ritualistic metaphor for time when he writes, "For I am already being poured out like a drink offering, and the time has come for my departure" (2 Timothy 4:6 NIV). For those who will remain alive after him, he encourages them to live with a sense of urgency; he wants them to live in the *kairos*, in the propitious moment, so that they will "[make] the most of the time" (Colossians 4:5). However, since all people, Christian or not, have ways of thinking about time that are chronological, ritualistic, or imperatival, the element that separates Christians from others is that Christians have ways of thinking about time that are cross-hatched by eschatology. Every moment of the Christian life is lived within the time-suspending and time-altering dimensions of the Advent, the Nativity, the Resurrection, and the Final Judgment. Out of the centuries of material available to us, four modern Christian prisoners—Kim Dae Jung, Alfred Delp, Dietrich Bonhoeffer, and Martin Luther King, Jr.—have much to teach us about how the voices of the imprisoned can guide our understanding of eschatology and the practice of hospitality.

Eschatology and Chronology

Kim Dae Jung won the Nobel Peace Prize in 2000 for his attempts to strengthen democracy in South Korea, but his early efforts at reform led to imprisonment. During this time, Kim, a Roman Catholic, wrote a series of letters to his family. His letters have not received much attention in theological circles but a close look at his writing reveals how close hospitality and eschatology are bound together.

Kim is not a trained theologian; his letters show him to be a sort of theological journeyman struggling with often difficult theological, biblical, and philosophical works. Like the apostle Paul, who asked Timothy to bring "the cloak that I left with Carpus at Troas, also the books, and above all the parchments" (2 Timothy 4:13), Kim often asked for reading material: his list included everything from Kant's *Critique of Practical Reason* to *Debates and Decrees of the Second Vatican Council*. He also read material by or about prisoners such as Aleksandr Solzhenitsyn's *Gulag Archipelago* and Henri Charriere's *Papillion*.[2] Both books show prison life at the extreme.

The chronological aspects of his letters are in some ways typical of all letters from prison. There are innocuous details like changes in the rain.[3] He worries about his wife's hay fever.[4] He encourages his children to study for their exams.[5] He frets about a child's refusal to go to the beach while he is in prison.[6] He is affectionate and says that his letters are "my way of expressing concern for you."[7] In a moving passage, Kim summons up a powerful image when he says of his monthly letter: "The letter goes home in my place, passing through the front gate, walking down the steps, entering the porch, and finally going into the living room to sit with the whole family."[8]

Suffering, Invisibility, and the Neighbor

Since Kim wants his letters to be events that take the place of his actual presence at this moment in chronological time, what does he want them to accomplish? First of all, Kim wants his letters to be practical forms of encouragement for others who are suffering. He wants others to take his letters as an encouragement to be *audible* on his behalf, to speak for him. This is quite risky since some of Kim's associates, like those in Kwangju demonstrations, are being persecuted.[9] Nevertheless, he quite often closes a letter by saying, "Do not forget about those who are suffering on our account, and remember to console and encourage them, if only spiritually. I hope you will do this on my behalf."[10] Or he can broaden his appeal by including family members: "Do not forget to thank and console those who are suffering on our account. This goes for their families as well. On behalf of your father, please carry this out with utmost sincerity."[11] He makes sure to stress that this must be done in his name: "As I always say, my heart aches whenever I think of my brothers and close colleagues and the great hardship and suffering I have caused them. I pray to Jesus for His blessing on them."[12]

Second, Kim wants his letters to help him remain *visible*. Because prisoners are often confined in isolated areas away from population centers, visits are rare and frustrated by delays and sudden changes in administrative policy. Even when prison is close at hand, visiting someone is prison is shameful and embarrassing. Because of this, prisoners slowly become both unheard and unseen. Kim battles against this by stressing to his family that they should break this pattern by looking again and differently at not only those who are in prison but also those who *are presently free.* For example, he counsels that every occasion offers an opportunity for prayer. While riding a bus, they should pray for the safety of fellow passengers. When crossing a street, they should pray for those at the intersection. He goes on to include those who work in restaurants, those at school, and those on dates.[13] Kim's effort here is to make the neighbor visible.

Invisibility is a major detriment to the practice of hospitality in urban areas. Because we encounter dozens or hundreds of people each day, everyone becomes a stranger to us. What Kim rightly saw is that this same urbanization that brings more and more people into contact with one another actually threatens our sense of belonging to a community. We begin to be *surrounded* by others but we no longer see ourselves as *with* others. Kim feels this has to be overcome. His recommendations about prayer are the first attempt at seeing what we really see all the time. He says in one letter, "It would be false to say one can love an invisible God when one cannot even love one's neighbors, God's children, who are, after all, quite visible."[14]

Kim makes the neighbor, and by this the prisoner, visible by speaking of misplaced love of oneself and love of God and one's neighbors. Misplaced love of self is "selfish, isolating, and demeaning"; love of the Creator and the neighbor "leads to happiness and eternal life."[15] This is one of the bases for Kim's admonition to his son Hong-gul, who is preparing to decide his major in college. Hong-gul appears to share the typical aspirations and desires of many teenagers. Automobiles, the martial arts, and athletics fascinate him. Kim does not downplay these interests and commends him for his tenacity in pursuing these interests. However, Kim then adds the following admonition:

> You do of course have shortcomings. One is a seeming lack of concern for neighbors, but I know that if you patiently cultivate the strengths I have mentioned, you are sure to find happiness and success. I hope that you proceed toward the goals in your life with humility before God and neighbors and with a mental attitude that remains positive.[16]

This is fatherly advice, but at the same time Kim is concerned with the formation of character—a character that overcomes selfish desires. It is the sign of the presence of the kingdom of God. He says to his daughter-in-law:

> I believe our lives will be most meaningful if we spend them by participating with Him in the task whose aim is to bring about the days when God's will is done in this world as in heaven. For this end, as children of God, we must dedicate ourselves to the twofold purpose of individual and social salvation; that is, we must help our neighbors and devote ourselves to the betterment of our society. We must synchronize and harmonize these two enterprises just like the two wheels of an ox-cart.[17]

INCARNATION AND RESURRECTION

Kim's theology of love of neighbor is grounded in his understanding of two eschatological events: the Incarnation and the Resurrection. There is no doubt for him of the historical validity of these events.[18] The two events are significant markers of the interruption of human ways of telling time. He calls eschatology a "revolutionary idea" that broke through the recurring cycle of birth and death. The two events of the Incarnation and the Resurrection have great significance for the present as we lean into the future. He argues that because of these two events "tomorrow would not be just another day."[19]

According to Kim, it is through the Resurrection that God gives us hope and demonstrates God's love. The Resurrection is no mere event in the past; Kim believes that the Resurrection is an ongoing event. In a letter to his son, Kim points to how this event transcends time, indeed changes it. He says, "Through Jesus' resurrection, God gave us hope for eternal life. God is with you at this very moment."[20] Realizing this brings a new orientation toward others, Kim stresses the importance of hospitality when he says:

> Our neighbors are all God's children, whether they are Christians or not. It is only natural that we love those who are our brothers before God. To love especially those of our neighbors who need our care and encouragement is one of the most important of God's commandments. And when we consider how much loving care we receive from others, in food, shelter, clothing, education, health, and other ways, loving them is only a fitting return for all the love they have given us.[21]

So central is the Resurrection that Kim can use it to tie together his complete view of hospitality. He writes:

> We should pay more attention, however, to a fact made clear in the Bible: He was executed as a political prisoner by the Jewish ruling class and the Roman Empire for standing up for the rights of the oppressed and the poor. His resurrection, therefore, *should not be*

(emphasis added) interpreted simply as hope for eternal life in heaven. It should be seen as God's approval and confirmation of Christ's actions on earth, that is, as a sign of God's approval for Jesus' struggle and advocacy of justice and peace in this world, which should be made unconditionally accessible to the oppressed and the poor.[22]

In Kim's letters we find a witness to one way in which chronological time has to be rethought.

ALFRED DELP AND DIETRICH BONHOEFFER ON RITUALISTIC/LITURGICAL APPROACHES TO TIME

The season of Advent is the four weeks before Christmas. It is a period of anticipation and expectation while Christians wait for the Nativity, the birth of Jesus. But it also looks beyond the birth of Jesus to his Second Coming. It is preparation for his return. As such, the period of Advent has deep eschatological significance; Advent reminds Christians that they live "between the times." They live after the Resurrection but before the end of days. This eschatological component is reflected by the selection of Romans 13:11-14 as one of the readings for the first Sunday. The first two verses read: "Besides this, you know what time it is, how it is now the moment for you to wake from sleep. For salvation is nearer to us now than when we became believers; the night is far gone, the day is near."

Like the orders of the medieval monasteries that called for daily offices of prayer, the contemporary liturgical Christian seeks to find in the coming and passing of Sundays a rhythm that provides order for the months of life. When the Nazis imprisoned the young Jesuit priest Alfred Delp for allegations of participation in treasonous affairs, he began a diary and a series of letters to his friends and family that reveal the potency of this rhythm in the face of impending death. Among his writings are a series of meditations on Advent. In these, Delp puts himself deeply into liturgical time and considered the meditations to be a gift to his reader. He writes, "Its purpose is not good prose but an exposition of truth which we must refer to again and again as a standard and a source of encouragement when the burden of these dreadful days becomes too heavy and confusing."[23]

The dreadful days that Delp refers to are those of the constant bombing by the Allied forces. He chooses to subvert the rattling explosions by reminding himself, from the perspective of eschatology, that Advent is a time of rousing that shakes humanity and wakens us to the truth about ourselves.[24] He chooses to view the days through meditations on the "symbols" of Advent: the call of John the Baptist, the announcement of the herald angel, and Mary the Blessed Lady. John the Baptist calls out that although we live in a wilderness, God promises to "clear away [the] bomb dust and rubble of destruction, making the rough places clear again."[25] The angel reminds us that the horror of life is counteracted by the quiet and unseen way God proclaims good news to those who are "so immured within the four walls of their prison that their very eyes are dimmed, they see nothing but grey days through barred windows placed too high to see out of."[26] Finally, Delp sees in the symbol of Mary one who in her pregnancy "knows how to wait" until the last hour has come.[27] These are three voices crying out above the violence, destruction, and false clamor of the days.[28] Hearing them makes life a continuous Advent; living by the liturgical calendar and not the calendar of the world gives one the resources needed to rise above the current crisis.

There is a section in Bonhoeffer's writings that reflects the same ideas as Delp. It is written from Tegel Prison during the first week of Advent, November 1943:

Although I don't know how letters are getting through at present, I want to write to you on the afternoon of the First Sunday in Advent. Altdorfer's "Nativity" is very topical this year, showing the Holy Family and the crib among the ruins of a tumbledown house. How ever did he come to paint like that, against all tradition, four hundred years ago? Perhaps he meant that Christmas could and should be kept even in such conditions; in any case, that is his message for us. I like to think of your sitting with the children and keeping Advent with them, just as you used to years ago with us. Only we do everything more intensively now, as we don't know how much longer we have.[29]

I have already pointed out the tremulous nature of prisoners' letters. Bonhoeffer echoes this here; perhaps his letters are delayed or destroyed. They are subject to war, whim, and weather. He keeps on writing in spite of these uncertainties.

The painting Bonhoeffer refers to, Albrecht Altdorfer's *Nativity* is an astonishing painting that is a graphic depiction of eschatology.[30] Contemporary with Albrecht Dürer, Lucas Cranach, and Hans Holbein, Altdorfer was proficient in the major media of his time (painting, woodcuts, and etchings). As one of the first persons in European art to paint independent landscapes, he chose mountains, cliffs, rivers, and streambeds; and when he included persons, they were often reduced to tiny, anonymous figures. Yet, in *Nativity* the figures are neither small nor anonymous: they are proportional to the setting, neither dominating nor retreating.

The compelling item in the painting is the depiction of the house and stable as a ruin. Altdorfer carefully places two sides of a remaining wall in the center of the frame. A good portion of the wall is already rubble; the remaining is uneven, with missing bricks and crumbling mortar. The house has decayed and shows its exposed beams, rough and missing counter support. Jesus, Mary, and Joseph are behind the teetering corner of a wall and underneath, in the cellar of the rotting building.

We are lead to consider the meaning of shelter. No human construction survives the assault of time. The lone animal in the painting has no sense of the season. One day is as another. But the cherubs, who flutter above and who have come to adore by watching, and who represent the intersection of the transcendent and the local, are heralds of a new moment in time. Altdorfer asks the viewer of the painting to see "the signs of the times" not just in the contrast between the cherubs and the ox, but also in the strong contrast between two atmospheric conditions. He paints an ominous and threatening sky, thick and black, covering three-fifths of the upper portion of the canvas. But the forbidding clouds are punctured, almost blasted away, by a sun of outsized proportions. Round and pulsating, the sun symbolizes the day of revelation, the new beginning, the advent of the new world already emerging. It is not in the position of noon, but coming into the horizon at eleven o'clock and will, we can be assured, push away the symbols of the old age.

Bonhoeffer's words now become clear. Against all tradition, Altdorfer has used landscape as a theological narrative that is ripe with eschatology. It is "topical" for Bonhoeffer, because for him this Advent season is one of ruin and destruction. Like Delp, he lives in the midst of ruin. The bombing is constant and never far away. Reports of new calamities reach the prison daily. Sometimes the prisoners cannot even hear one another, presumably because of the aftereffects of concussions. In a touch of humor, he notes that even exercise in the prison yard, a luxury for prisoners and one of the few places where time becomes normal again, has had to be called off because the prison walls have been broken.[31] Altdorfer's work shows Bonhoeffer that even amid such despair and destruction, Advent must be kept. The Christian must live in the times but must do so in a way that is consonant with that which is above the times.

Martin Luther King, Jr., and a Kairotic Approach to Time

There is perhaps not a single letter in American history that has had a greater impact on the consciousness of the nation than Martin Luther King, Jr.'s "Letter from Birmingham Jail." The letter has a careful and balanced rhetoric; its structure and style is elegant, but the real power of the letter is in its eschatology. Moreover, hospitality and eschatology are tied together right at the start of the text.

In the opening chapter of *Why We Can't Wait,* the book that came to contain the final edition of "Letter from Birmingham Jail," King refers to the slow pace at which federal plans to bring about desegregation were moving. He says:

> While Negros were being appointed to some significant jobs, and
> social hospitality was being extended at the White House to Negro

leaders, the dreams of the masses remained in tatters. The Negro felt that he recognized the same old bone that had been tossed to him in the past—only now it was being handed to him on a platter with courtesy.[32]

King refers to "social hospitality." The phrase "social hospitality" hides as much as it reveals. King's meeting with President Kennedy on June 22, 1963, had been long sought. Both had pressed each other for a meeting prior to this, but the meeting had been delayed or denied by both sides while they gauged the relative political advantages the meeting offered. When the meeting did occur, King found himself captive to the scheduling office of the White House, which cleverly had King meet with the president on a weekend morning after Kennedy had met with Roy Wilkins, executive secretary of the NAACP at that time, and immediately before a meeting with other national leaders concerned with civil rights. This avoided the appearance that Kennedy was granting any particular importance to King.[33] When King did meet privately with the president it was turned into a tour of the Rose Garden and a furtive discussion on King's association with alleged "agents of a foreign power."[34] When King recalls the meeting with the phrase "social hospitality" it is perhaps a gentle way of saying that courtesy is not the same as conviction. In any case, King is pressing home the point that the time for action has arrived.

In "Letter from Birmingham Jail," King offers six refutations of the argument made by eight Alabama clergymen that his activities in Birmingham were "unwise and untimely." The clergymen's letter was published in the local newspaper as an open letter in anticipation of the coming protests. As representatives of the white religious community they positioned themselves as moderates who thought that the negotiation over civil matters was best left to run its course and that confrontation should wait its day. King became aware of the letter while he was in jail and began crafting his response on the margins of the newspaper smuggled in to him by a sympathetic jailer. With the assistance of Wyatt Tee Walker, King wrote and rewrote his response over the next twenty-four hours. It was an epochal moment. By using the public media, King was echoing the eschatological command given to the ancient prophet Habakkuk:

> Write the vision;
>> make it plain upon tablets,
>> so he may run who reads it.
> For still the vision awaits its time. (Habakkuk 2:2-3 RSV)

The six refutations are as follows: the demonstrations were necessary because negotiations had failed; waiting longer would not curtail the humiliation of segregation now; their actions were in line with the idea of just and unjust laws; the demonstrators could not be blamed for precipitating violence because their claims were just; it is irrational to believe that "the very flow of time will inevitably cure all ills"; and discontent with the status quo is not equivalent with extremism.

These objections to the clergy's letter are imbued with an eschatological perspective of time. Turning away from negotiation and toward direct action is buttressed by a reappraisal of the creative uses of tension.[35] There is reason to believe that an increase in tension should be viewed as a welcome harbinger of change. Whereas the past period has been dominated by the stagnancy of the status quo, King's belief is that the Negro can only be heard if the past and present are swept away by the life-giving power of the future. The idea that the demonstrations are untimely is countered by the phrase, "We are sadly mistaken if we feel that the election of Albert Boutwell as mayor will bring the millennium to Birmingham."[36] The clergy's concern that laws are being broken is set aside by King's claim that at every point in time one must constantly reflect on the immediacy of obedience to God.[37] As for precipitating violence, King borrows the Christology of F. D. E. Schleiermacher and through it counters that Jesus' unique "God-consciousness" allows Christians to act in ways that protect the robbed and punish the robber.[38] Instead of waiting for change, he argues that "the time is always ripe" to do what is right.[39] The charge of extremism is erased by an appeal to the *zeitgeist* brought about through the current changes in political affairs in Asia, South America, and other parts of the globe.[40] The refutations of the clergymen's letter may have been written in a twenty-four-hour period, but the theology behind it was long in development.

KING'S TWOFOLD ESCHATOLOGICAL PERSPECTIVE

The biblical text most widely associated with Martin Luther King, Jr., is Amos 5:24: "Let justice roll down like waters, and righteousness like an ever-flowing stream." King's realization of the significance of this text was clear to him at least as early as January of 1953 while he was in his doctoral studies at Boston University. King had a habit of making note cards on biblical texts for himself and he commented on the Amos passage: "Amos' emphasis throughout seems to be that justice between man and man is one of the divine foundations of society. Such an ethical ideal is at the root of all true religion. This high ethical notion conceived by Amos must alway [sic] remain a challenge to the Christian church."[41] It is impossible now to consider King apart from the Amos passage; however, it is important to understand that another biblical passage was also fundamental for him: the parable of the sheep and the goats.[42]

King gave serious thought to the parable of the sheep and the goats while he was at Crozer Theological Seminary in 1950. In a class exam for "Christian Theology for Today," King wrestles with how to interpret the Second Coming. He rejects a pure literalism that requires believing in a "pre-scientific world view which we cannot accept."[43] Instead, King sees in the Second Coming and in the Day of Judgment the idea that "The final doctrine of the second coming is that whenever we turn our lives to the highest and best there for us is the Christ."[44] This is a dismissal of traditional Protestant teaching on the last days with its emphasis on a literal physical return. King's point of view is more along the lines of a symbolized eschatology: encountering Jesus occurs for every believer not in the future but in the present, and continually so. He goes on to say:

We must agree with the spiritual value of this view held by the early Christians, for the personality of Jesus does serve as a judgment upon us all. When we set aside the spectacular paraphernalia of the judgment scene and the literal throne we come to the real meaning of the doctrine. The highest court of justice is in the heart of man after the light of Christ has illumined his motive and all his inner life. Any day when {we} waken to the fact that we are making a great moral decision, any day of experienced nearness to Christ . . . we see ourselves, is a day of judgment.[45]

King's rejection of literalism in relationship to eschatology should not surprise us since King had rejected a literal resurrection of Jesus during a Sunday school class when he was only thirteen. His studies at Morehouse College and Crozer Theological Seminary gave his position more substance.[46] This more "mature" view of the Second Coming came from his engagement with George Hedley's *Symbol of the Faith*.[47] Hedley's thesis, adopted by King, is that

in order to understand the meaning and the significance of any doctrine or creed it is necessary to study the experiences of the individuals that produced them. Doctrines and creeds do not spring forth uncaused like Athene sprang from the head of Zeus, but they grow out of the historical settings and the psychological moods of the individuals that set them forth.[48]

The attempt to determine the experiential origin of Christian teaching was the fruit of German scholars such as Adolph von Harnack who set into motion the historical criticism of church doctrine. In this case, King's demythologizing, so to speak, is joined with the social gospel of Walter Rauschenbusch. This comes out clearly in another essay from King's Crozer days in which he explains that in the history of Christianity, the meaning of the kingdom of God has always had a social emphasis; it might be theocratic, or triumphalist, or apocalyptic, but

here we are left in no doubt as to the true meaning of the concept. Whether it come soon or late, by sudden crisis of [sic] through slow development, the kingdom of God will be a society in which all men and women will be controlled by the eternal love of God. When we see social relationships controlled everywhere by the priciples [sic] which Jesus illustrated in his life—trust, love, mercy, and altruism—then we shall know that the kingdom of God is here. To say what this society will be like in exact detail is quite hard for us to picture, for it runs so counter to the practices of our present social life. But we can rest assured that it will be a society governed by the law of love.[49]

King wrote those words in the relative comfort of Chester, Pennsylvania. A test of how much he believed them came in Montgomery, Alabama. On December 2, 1955, the Women's Political Council in Montgomery circulated a leaflet calling for a one-day boycott of city buses on December 5 and urging citizens to be in attendance at Holt Street Baptist Church where "further instruction" would be given.[50] On the afternoon of the announced day, Martin Luther King, Jr., was elected president of the newly formed Montgomery Improvement Association during a meeting at Mount Zion AME Zion Church. It was agreed that he would speak that evening along with songs and prayers and the reading of the recommendations and resolutions developed by the executive committee. The agenda called for King to address the crowd in two parts. He used the first part to welcome the crowd and to set out the justifying themes for their assembly: the rights of citizenship, the needs of justice, and the fortunes of democracy. He stressed that the protesters were "a Christian people" making their appeal based on the notion that "justice is love correcting that which revolts against love."[51] It is in this context that King quotes Amos 5:24:

And we are not wrong, we are not wrong in what we are doing. If we are wrong, the Supreme Court of this nation is wrong. If we are wrong, the Constitution of the United States is wrong. If we are wrong, God Almighty is wrong. If we are wrong, Jesus of Nazareth was merely a utopian dreamer that never came down to earth. If we are wrong, justice is a lie. Love has no meaning. And we are determined here in Montgomery to work and fight until justice runs down like water, and righteousness like a mighty stream.[52]

At this point, King stopped and turned the podium over to Rosa Parks, E. N. French, and Ralph Abernathy. When they finished, King returned and gave the second half of his address. He began by commending the meeting for passing the resolutions put before them, telling them that some practical problems would have to be addressed if the bus boycott was to work, and then he said:

> And we will not be content until oppression is wiped out of Montgomery, and really out of America. We won't be content until that is done. We are merely insisting on the dignity and worth of every human personality. And I don't stand here, I'm not arguing for any selfish person. I've never been on a bus in Montgomery. But I would be less than a Christian if I stood back and said, because I don't ride the bus, I don't have to ride a bus, that it doesn't concern me. I will not be content. I can hear a voice saying, "If you do it unto the least of these, my brother, you do it unto me." [53]

King's statement that he had never ridden the buses in Montgomery should be startling to anyone today who thinks of the bus boycott as a national event and a turning point in American social history. At his trial three months later for breaking the antiboycott law, he said on direct examination that since his arrival in Montgomery in 1954 he had only ridden the buses once.[54] King owned a car well before coming to Montgomery, and as the minister of the Dexter Avenue Baptist Church owning a car was a social and practical necessity. What we should note is that although the experience of racial discrimination was never far from anyone's daily experience during the time of the segregated South, in a strange way many people, like King in this case, never routinely experienced its subtleties. King could not doubt the reality of what happened to others but he was, however, not subject to this particular insult. In the face of all the other indignities he had to endure, from a purely personal point of view, discrimination on the buses was hardly among the chief of his concerns.

King takes the point of view that it is his concern because he is impelled by the injunction of Matthew 25:40. He is part of a larger community; he is a Christian, and the Word of God has challenged him in personal way. This same point of view is echoed by Coretta Scott King in her statement to the press a year later after her husband's conviction for violating the antiboycott law: "All along I have supported my husband in this cause and at this point I feel even stronger about the cause, and whatever happens to him it happens to me." [55] Whereas her statement could be understood only as a wife's loyal support, it should be understood as something much deeper. The foundation of the Civil Rights movement was in every way impelled by a commitment to public hospitality founded in an understanding of eschatology.

On February 4, 1968, almost five years after the Birmingham imprisonment, King gave a sermon at Ebenezer Baptist Church in Atlanta, Georgia, entitled "The Drum Major Instinct." Most of the sermon was borrowed from a Florida preacher named J. Wallace Hamilton and, as Keith Miller points out, the tradition of borrowing and adapting the sermons of others has always been a feature of African American preaching.[56] Given the fact that Hamilton had published the sermon as a pamphlet it certainly was adapted by many others besides King. What is very significant, however, is the way King appends his own conclusion. The transcript of the audiotape is as follows:

> If any of you are around when I have to meet my day, I don't want a long funeral. And if you get somebody to deliver the eulogy, tell them not to talk too long. (*Yes*) And every now and then I wonder what I want them to say. Tell them not to mention that I have a Nobel Peace Prize—that isn't important. Tell them not to mention that I have three or four hundred other awards—that's not important. Tell them not to mention where I went to school. (*Yes*)
>
> I'd like somebody to mention that day that Martin Luther King, Jr., tried to give his life serving others. (*Yes*)
>
> I'd like for somebody to say that day that Martin Luther King, Jr., tried to love somebody.
>
> I want you to say that day that I tried to be right on the war question. (*Amen*)
>
> I want you to be able to say that day that I did try to feed the hungry. (*Yes*)

And I want you to be able to say that day that I did try in my life to clothe those who were naked. *(Yes)*

I want you to say on that day that I did try in my life to visit those who were in prison. *(Lord)*

I want you to say that I tried to love and serve humanity. *(Yes)*

Yes, if you want to say that I was a drum major, say that I was a drum major for justice. *(Amen)* Say that I was a drum major for peace. *(Yes)* I was a drum major for righteousness. And all of the other shallow things will not matter. *(Yes)* I won't have any money to leave behind. I won't have the fine and luxurious things of life to leave behind. But I just want to leave a committed life behind. *(Amen)* And that's all I want to say.[57]

King uses three rhetorical elements in this conclusion. First, King invites the present listener to become his future messenger ("If you get somebody . . . tell them"). Second, he uses negation and affirmation: tell them not to mention; tell them to mention. Third, King changes from the impersonal "somebody" to the highly personal "you." The listener is encouraged to take up the mantle of the prophet as he is falling, not just when he has fallen. Moreover, King wants those who are listening to see that what he did was not a matter of convenience but of conviction. There is a humility in the repeated statement "I tried to be right" that indicates that his actions did not come easily. It is most telling that King's speech couples his decision to oppose the Vietnam War, a decision that made him hugely unpopular, with his actions toward the hungry, the naked, and the imprisoned. When we add all of this together, we see that King viewed the Matthew 25 passage as a text that gave sufficient instruction on how to live even when his time for living was nearly past.

Though their circumstances were unique in many ways, King, Delp, Bonhoeffer, and Kim each saw a close relationship between hospitality and eschatology. Because they wrote letters, they each serve us by making us aware of how prison life is really and finally corrective. Their experiences should persuade us that prison life is eschatological *in toto* both for those who are imprisoned and for those who visit the imprisoned. The simple distinction between a visitor's time and a prisoner's time is enough to see this. The visitor's time is marked by waiting to get in; the prisoner's by waiting to get out.

Visiting someone in prison is an unpleasant and tedious affair. However, for the person who is in prison, a visit is an interruption, or better yet a disturbance of time so that it is transformed from chronological to kairotic. And although there are exceptions (one thinks of some prisons in South America and Asia, where visitors can even live with the imprisoned), the very nature of visiting a prisoner is incarnational and therefore eschatological: the visitor becomes enfleshed and the prisoner reembodied.

Chapter Five

Hospitality

THE PRACTICE BY WHICH THE CHURCH STANDS OR FALLS?

THE FOUNDATION OF HOSPITALITY

A colleague of mine, and a great wit, pointed out to me that the ancient Hellenists uncharitably characterized long books as a "great evil." Admittedly, they wrote better books than I have, but I hope that others will allow me the favor of assuming that brevity is still a virtue. I have demonstrated how Christian hospitality is founded in Christology, ecclesiology, reconciliation, and eschatology and argue that this gives it a distinctive purpose that its secular counterpart cannot have. To be sure, I have not at all covered anything close to a complete roster of the major Christian doctrines. We spent no time contemplating how understanding the Eucharist as a shared meal is fundamental to all aspects of the Christian life. In the same way, a proper understanding of the Trinity would make clear that hospitality draws upon the mutual sharing of the persons of the Trinity with one another. But even when we have said all that could be said, if it was at all possible to do so, we must contend with the insurmountable fact that in the end hospitality is a practice—an action—and actions are dependent upon will. When Paul admonishes in Romans 12:13 to "contribute to the needs of the saints; extend hospitality to strangers," he first establishes that we should not "be conformed to this world, but be transformed by the renewing of [our] minds, so that [we] may discern what is the will of God—what is good and acceptable and perfect" (Romans 12:2).

Our study throughout has tried to push ever deeper into the parable of the sheep and the goats. It has been the basis and the limit of the work. Yet, what does the parable say about the will to be hospitable? We face a great turning point when we notice that those gathered around the throne are clearly startled by their acceptance or their rejection. The basis for this amazement is being told that they either did or did not see Jesus in the face of the stranger. Those who object to the decision of the King do not excuse themselves by saying that they were willing to serve, nor do they offer excuses that they found the task unpleasant, or demanding, or even demeaning. They do not cry out that the tasks before them were too hard, that resources were lacking. They do not ask for a second chance. Rather, we find that their protest is simply that they did not see: "When did we see you hungry or thirsty or a stranger or naked or sick or in prison?"

It must be asserted, then, that in regard to hospitality the will to serve only comes after one is conditioned to seeing. Careful readers of the gospel would not be surprised by this, for the evangelists make it known from the earliest chapters that what distinguished Jesus, what made him a curiosity, then notable and famous, was his remarkable ability to see. Jesus was blessed with perfect sight. Whether it is with Peter's mother-in-law, the woman with the incurable hemorrhage, the hungry crowd, or the boy with seizures, in each case the narratives pause to lay emphasis on the fact that Jesus *saw*. It was sight that moved his will.

Even more remarkably, and of very great importance, is the fact that in these cases, as in so many others, Jesus does not set out to see. That is, he does not go looking for someone to heal, or someone to deliver. Jesus' hospitality to the displaced and distressed was not calculated but casual. It is as though Jesus lived his life as a type of present participle: as he was going, Jesus saw.

It is this casualness that undercuts much of what goes by the name of Christian hospitality today. The churches of the country continue to promote program after program, and call committee after committee, to care for the poor, the naked, and the hungry. There is merit, of course, in organization. There is something good to be done by working together. But these efforts, as noble as they are, begin the process of institutionalizing care. When that happens, our ability to see the stranger "as we are going" is eroded. Clothing and feeding, welcoming and visiting, become agendas. By adopting the vision of Jesus, by seeing as and how Jesus sees, our inclination toward hospitality will become natural and unforced. Hospitality ought to be ad hoc and personal.

If there is something to be gained from observing what those around the throne say, then there is also something to be gained by observing what the One who speaks from the throne says. The King says: "Come, you that are blessed by my Father, inherit the kingdom prepared for you from the foundation of the world" (Matthew 25:34). In the Old Testament the phrase "from the foundation of the world" reflects an ancient mythology that viewed the earth as set upon pillars, with God pictured as the architect of all that is built (Job 38:4; Psalms 78:69; 102:25; 104:9; Isaiah 48:13). When Jesus then speaks of the Kingdom as a place whose origin coincides with the "the foundation of the world," it indicates that for Jesus hospitality is fundamental to the very being of God.

Moreover, Jesus is explicit that the Kingdom is inherited. Inheritance is one of the critical concepts of biblical life; the entire structure and success of the nation of Israel turned upon the critical idea of land and place being passed along through family lines (Genesis 15:2; Exodus 32:13; Numbers 27:1-11; 36:7; and so forth). "Inherit" suggests a complete turning over, a willing, of house and property. The stranger, the widow, and the orphan are in peril; they are in need of hospitality, because they have been disinherited in one sense or another. One passage, 1 Samuel 2:7-8 (NIV), brings this all together rather well:

> The LORD sends poverty and wealth;
>   he humbles and he exalts.
> He raises the poor from the dust
>   and lifts the needy from the ash heap;
> he seats them with princes
>   and has them inherit a throne of honor.
> "For the foundations of the earth are the
>   LORD's;
>   upon them he has set the world."

We are given here a glimpse at the mind of God, at the essence of God. The God who sees the end from the beginning has always envisioned that the goal of creation was homecoming, welcoming, and receiving. Toward this goal God structures God's life around the activity of preparation: God sees what is needed and God wills to make it happen.

MISSION IS THE MOTHER OF COMPASSION

"You will be my witnesses in Jerusalem, in all Judea and Samaria, and to the ends of the earth" (Acts 1:8). These are the opening words of the Acts of the Apostles and they indicate that Christian mission is synonymous with travel. This does not surprise close readers of Luke's writings because Luke has already stressed that the crossing of geographical borders continually marked Jesus' mission (Luke 4:37; 8:26; 8:37; 17:1). Luke does not ever depict Jesus as a tourist. Rather, he is shown to be a pilgrim (Luke 12:41) who takes an interest in the people he observes along his route (Luke 21:1). He marvels only at people's unbelief and never over physical attractions (Luke 21:5-6).

Jesus belonged to that group of people whose travel is intentional. He left the north and traveled south with his face set toward Jerusalem (Luke 9:51). And although Luke is not like Matthew, who explains Jesus' early life as refugee in Egypt, Luke is clear that it is Jesus' insistence on crossing the border from Galilee into Judea that caused the outrage of his religious opponents and that this led to his death (Luke 23:5).

Purposeful and freely chosen travel is the result of will: adventurers, immigrants, tourists, and missionaries have this in common.[1] They are distinct from the refugee, the exile, and the kidnapped, because they are voluntary travelers. They do not have a sense that they are being taken from a place they wanted to be to a place they do not want to be. They are freely electing to cross borders. They are not forced, evicted, or chased by war, famine, or natural disaster. They anticipate the future in a way that others do not. In conjunction with this, they travel joyfully even when they come into situations that have the prospect of danger.

But it is important to note that although missionaries belong to a common group, those who are engaged in mission are distinct from the tourist, the adventurer, and the immigrant in this way: for the missionary, crossing a border is a transcendent act. It is not merely a matter of self-fulfillment, actualization, or leisure. It is an imitation of the God who came near. This means that they have a distinctly different appreciation of borders and boundaries.

Consider the following. The person who crosses a border sees the border as a sign or symbol usually designating some form of limit. This is clear when the borders are geographic. The river, the mountain, and the ocean all may designate the end of one area and the beginning of another. Yet, visible geographic borders are established and reenforced by unseen social, political, religious, psychological, historical, sexual, and anthropological conventions or decrees. The character of crossing a visible, marked, and known geographical border—the river for example—is different from crossing a social, political, or religious border. Moreover, borders are multivalent. There is never a single border that is crossed in any event. The crossing of a geographical border brings with it an encounter with other types of borders. Going "into Africa," for example, is going into multiple bordered worlds, each with a landscape and terrain of its own. The variances we encounter evoke a different response, each in turn. To complicate matters even more, borders and the crossing of borders are events of which we may not be conscious. If you wade through a river and the river designates a known border, you are immediately aware of what you have done because you are wet.

The missionary does and experiences all of the above but adds the factor of intending to disrupt and intending to disenchant those who are met once over the border. The missionary, and this is what makes missionary work both so attractive and so dangerous, seeks to both break allegiances to old or false borders and to announce the circumscription of all things in Christ. The adventurer, the tourist, and even the migrant say, "Let me visit briefly. Let me climb this rock, or see this building, or even tend this farm, and then by and by, I will be away." The missionary is never so agreeable, never so willing to pet and stroke. This is what makes missionaries able to see, really see, those they encounter.

It is convicting to me that the Gospel writers used the rare word *splagchnizomai* to describe what Jesus felt when he encountered those on the margins (Matthew 20:34; Mark 1:41; 8:2; Luke 7:13). Greek speakers understood the word to mean "to be moved as to one's bowels." We would speak of "a feeling in the gut," but it is difficult to give an adequate translation of the word. Jesus uses it once in speaking about forgiveness (the parable of the unforgiving servant, Matthew 18:21) and, significantly, twice in parables associated with hospitality (the good Samaritan and the prodigal son). More broadly, the Gospel writers want us to see that Jesus took into himself the pain and "dis-ease" of those on the borders of life. In this age where feeling another's pain is either a tagline of the trite or mimicry of the mightless, we cannot let compassion become casual.

I once saw a picture of a young hitchhiker as she stood on the island of a busy street. Tall and gaunt, she bore the weary expression that we so often see carried by those who feel themselves on the margins of life. Clumped beside her feet were her bound possessions that appeared as rumpled as what she wore. All of this was, unfortunately, rather ordinary. Folk of her band are as common as the cars that passed her by. What made the picture compelling was the sign she held. Written on a piece of cardboard was the word *Anywhere.* She asked not for Los Angeles, New York, or Miami. She asked not for home or to be taken away from home.

All of this was a road too far. She simply asked, dare I say begged, to be taken not away, but in. If this is the case, that she wanted to be taken in and not just away, then she represents those who Jesus calls us to see. Hospitality is the practice by which the church stands or falls.

Notes

INTRODUCTION: THROWING UP IN WYNNEWOOD

1. Karl Barth, *Church Dogmatics* III/3, ed. and trans. G. W. Bromiley and T. F. Torrance (Edinburgh: T & T Clark, 1960), 415.

2. Tertullian, "To His Wife," in *Ante-Nicene Fathers*, vol. IV, ed. Phillip Schaff and James Donaldson (New York: Hendrickson Publishers, 1994), 39-49.

3. Gregory the Great, "Epistle III, To Janurius, Bishop of Caralis," in *Nicene and Post-Nicene Fathers*, 2nd series, vol. XIII, ed. Philip Schaff and Henry Wace (Peabody, MA: Hendrickson Publishers, 1994), 1-2.

4. Martin Luther, "Whether One May Flee from a Deadly Plague," in *Martin Luther's Theological Writings*, ed. Timothy F. Lull (Minneapolis: Fortress Press, 1989), 736-55.

5. Robert W. Baldwin, "On Earth We Are Beggars, as Christ Himself Was: The Protestant Background of Rembrandt's Imagery of Poverty, Disability, and Begging," *Konsthistorik Tidskrift* 54, no. 3 (1985): 122-35.

6. Amy G. Oden, *And You Welcomed Me: A Sourcebook on Hospitality in Early Christianity* (Nashville: Abingdon Press, 2001); Christine D. Pohl, *Making Room: Recovering Hospitality as a Christian Practice* (Grand Rapids: Eerdmans, 1999). For the newer biblical studies see Brendan Byrne S.J., *The Hospitality of God: A Reading of Luke's Gospel* (Collegeville, MN: Liturgical Press, 2000); Michael F. Trainor, *The Quest for Home: The Household in Mark's Community* (Collegeville, MN: Liturgical Press, 2001). For philosophy see Jacques Derrida, *Of Hospitality*, trans. Rachel Bowlby (Stanford: Stanford University Press, 2000); Julia Kristeva, *Strangers to Ourselves*, trans. Leon S. Roudiez (New York: Columbia University Press, 1994); Emmanuel Levinas, *Alterity and Transcendence* (New York: Columbia University Press, 1999).

7. Delores S. Williams, *Sisters in the Wilderness: The Challenge of Womanist God-Talk* (Maryknoll, NY: Orbis, 1993).

8. John Paul II, *The Gospel of Life (Evangelium Vitae)* (New York: Random House, 1995), 72.

9. Ladislaus J. Bolchazy, *Hospitality in Early Rome: Livy's Concept of Its Humanizing Force* (Chicago: Ares Publishers, 1977).

10. David Gilmore, Editor, *Honor and Shame and the Unity of the Mediterranean* (Washington, DC: The American Anthropological Association, 1987); Julian Pitt-Rivers, "The Stranger, The Guest, and the Hostile Host," in *Contributions of Mediterranean Sociology*, ed. J. G. Peristiany (Paris: Mouton , 1968), 13-30; A. M. Abou Zeid, "Honour and Shame Among the Bedouin of Egypt," in *Honour and Shame: The Values of Mediterranean Society*, ed. J. G. Peristiany (London: Weidenfeld and Nicolson, 1965), 245-59.

1. "Poor, Wayfaring Stranger"

1. Thurman's theology also combines strands of Quaker mysticism and liberal theology, with black Baptist sensibility. One of the best interpreters of Thurman is Luther E. Smith Jr., *Howard Thurman: The Mystic as Prophet* (Richmond, IN: Friends United Press, 1991). See also Mozella G. Mitchell, ed., *The Human Search: Howard Thurman and the Quest for Freedom; Proceedings of the Second Annual Thurman Convocation*, Martin Luther King, Jr., Memorial Studies in Religion, Culture, and Social Development, vol. 1 (New York: Peter Lang, 1992).

2. Howard Thurman, *Deep River and The Negro Spiritual Speaks of Life and Death* (Richmond, IN: Friends United Press, 1975). *Negro Spiritual*, 11.

3. Thurman, *Negro Spiritual*, 12.

4. Ibid.

5. W. E. B. Du Bois, *The Souls of Black Folk* (New York: Bantam Books, 1989); Thurman, *Negro Spiritual*. There are a number of excellent interpretations of the spirituals besides those of Du Bois and Thurman. See John Lovell, *Black Song: The Forge and the Flame* (New York: Macmillan, 1972); James Cone, *The Spirituals and the Blues: An Interpretation* (New York: Seabury Press, 1972); Dena J. Epstein, *Sinful Tunes and Spirituals: Black Folk Music to the Civil War* (Urbana: University of Illinois Press, 1977); Arthur C. Jones, *Wade in the Water: The Wisdom of the Spirituals* (Maryknoll, NY: Orbis, 1993); Bruno Chenu, *The Trouble I've Seen: The Big Book of Negro Spirituals*, trans. Eugene V. LaPlante (Valley Forge, VA: Judson Press, 2003).

6. This verse is omitted in some manuscripts.

7. For a history of the genre, see Michael W. Harris, *The Rise of Gospel Blues: The Music of Thomas Andrew Dorsey in the Urban Church* (New York: Oxford University Press, 1994). See also Robert Darden, *People Get Ready! A New History of Black Gospel Music* (New York: Continuum, 2004).

8. John Wesley Work, *Folk Song of the American Negro* (Westport, CT: Greenwood Press, 1969), 45.

9. At a minimum "slave religion" is composed of traditional Christian thought, African tribal religion, American frontier revivalism, and the peculiarities of denominationalism. Guides to this maze are found in Dwight N. Hopkins, *Down, Up, and Over: Slave Religion and Black Theology* (Minneapolis: Augsburg Fortress, 2000); Albert J. Raboteau, *Slave Religion: "The Invisible Institution" in the Antebellum South* (New York: Oxford, 2004); and Mechal Sobel, *Trabelin' On: The Slave Journey to an Afro-Baptist Faith* (Princeton, NJ: Princeton University Press, 1988).

10. "The Social Band," in Erskine Peters, *Lyrics of the Afro-American Spiritual* (Westport, CT: Greenwood Press, 1993), 39.

11. "Sister Mary Had-a But One Child" in Roland Hayes, *My Songs: Aframerican Religious Folk Songs Arranged and Interpreted* (Boston: Little, Brown, 1948), 98-102. Quoted in Peters, *Lyrics*, 38.

12. "The Angels Are Watching Over Me," in Peters, *Lyrics*, 52.

13. "God Is a God," in Ibid., 63-64.

14. All of this, of course, goes back to the Frazier/Herskovits debate on the survival of "Africanisms" in the New World. See Melville Herskovits, *The Myth of the Negro Past* (Boston: Beacon Press, 1958); E. Franklin Frazier, *The Negro Church* (New York: Schocken Books, 1964); John Edward Phillips, "The African Heritage of White America," in *Africanisms in American Culture*, ed. Joseph Holloway (Bloomington: Indiana University Press, 1990); Raboteau, *Slave Religion*, 48-52, 54-60.

15. I am thankful to Martin O'Malley, S.J. for this suggestion.

16. "Sometimes I Feel Like a Motherless Child," in Peters, *Lyrics*, 40.

17. "Pilgrim's Story," in Ibid., 140.

18. "Hard Trials," in *Songs of Zion* (Nashville: Abingdon Press, 1981), 107.

19. Chenu, *Trouble*, 173.

20. Thurman, *Negro Spiritual*, 38.

21. Chenu acknowledges that "the Son of God made flesh is given a multitude of titles and that the four great moments of his life—his birth, ministry, passion, and resurrection—are all well accounted for." Chenu, *Trouble*, 173. Titles alone, however, do not make for a sufficient Christology as the legacy of nineteenth-century German liberalism bears out.

22. John Punshon, *Portrait in Grey: A Short History of the Quakers* (London: Quaker Home Service, 1984), 158-67.

23. Randy L. Maddox, *Responsible Grace: John Wesley's Practical Theology* (Nashville: Abingdon Press, 1994), 114-17.

24. "He's a Mighty Good Leader," in Peters, *Lyrics*, 69.

25. Frederick Bauerschmidt suggested this to me.

26. "This Is the Man," in Peters, *Lyrics*, 100.

27. "Going to Heaven," in Peters, *Lyrics*, 312. It seems to me that "trails" should be "tears"; perhaps this is a typographical error. It is fair, too, to question this song's relative age and the distinction between spirituals and poems. Another example of "high Christology" is "Prepare Me One Body." See Hayes, 96-97.

28. Du Bois, *Souls*, 178.

29. Ibid., 2.

30. Ibid., 11.

31. Dolan Hubbard, "Riddle Me This: Du Bois, the Sphinx, and the Crisis of Identity," in *W. E. B. Du Bois and Race: Essays Celebrating the Centennial Publication of The Souls of Black Folk*, ed. Chester J. Fontenot Jr. and Mary Alice Morgan (Macon, GA: Mercer University Press, 2001), 26-44.

32. Du Bois, *Souls*, 179.

33. Ibid., 160.

34. W. E. B. Du Bois, "The Souls of White Folk," in *Darkwater: Voices from Within the Veil* (Mineola, NY: Dover, 1999), 17.

35. Du Bois, *Souls*, 44

36. Ibid., 52.

37. David Levering Lewis, *W. E. B. Du Bois: Biography of a Race, 1868–1919* (New York: Henry Holt, 1993), 242-43.

38. W. E. B. Du Bois, "The Negro and Crime," in *The Complete Published Works of W. E .B. Du Bois*, ed. Herbert Aptheker, vol. 1 (1891–1909), *Writings by W. E. B. Du Bois in Periodicals Edited by Others* (Millwood, NY: Kraus-Thomson Organization, 1982), 59.

39. W. E .B. Du Bois, "The Black Man in the Revolution of 1914–1918," in *The Complete Published Works of W. E. B. Du Bois*, ed, Herbert Aptheker, vol. 1 (1911–1925), *Writings in Periodicals Edited by W. E. B. Du Bois: Selections from The Crisis* (Millwood, NY: Kraus-Thomson Organization, 1983), 176.

40. W. E. B. Du Bois, "Hopkinsville, Chicago and Idlewild," in Ibid., 305.

41. Du Bois, *Souls*, 106.

42. See W. E. B. Du Bois, "On Religion," in *Du Bois on Religion*, ed. Phil Zuckerman (New York: Alta Maria, 2000).

43. Ibid., 94-95.

44. Ibid., 95.

2. THE DEATH OF HOSTILITY

1. The saddest example of this is the case of Saartjie Baartmann (Sara Bartman), the so-called Hottentot Venus, whose body was exhibited at Paris Musée de l'Homme for 150 years. See Yvette Abrahams, "Images of Sara Bartman: Sexuality, Race, and Gender in Early-Nineteenth-Century Britain," in *Nation, Empire, Colony: Historicizing Gender and Race*, ed. Ruth Roach Pierson and Nupur Chaudhuri (Bloomington and Indianapolis: Indiana University Press, 1998), 220-36.

2. I. A. Dorner, *System of Christian Ethics*, ed. A. Dorner, trans. C. M. Mead and R. T. Cunningham (Edinburgh: T & T Clark, 1906), 170.

3. Ibid., 172.

4. Ibid., 173.

5. Ibid., 172.

6. Ann Coulter, "This Is War," *National Review Online*, September 13, 2001, http://www.nationalreview.com/coulter/coulter.shtml

7. Thomas F. Madden, *A Concise History of the Crusades* (Lanham, MD: Rowman & Littlefield, 1999).

8. Perhaps the best new study of the Crusades is Christopher Tyerman, *Fighting for Christendom: Holy War and the Crusades* (Oxford: Oxford University Press, 2005).

9. Karl Barth, *Church Dogmatics* IV/1, ed. and trans. G. W. Bromiley and T. F. Torrance (Edinburgh: T & T Clark, 1956), 361.

10. Ibid.

11. Ibid., 390.

12. Ibid., 244.

13. Karl Barth, *Ethics*, ed. Dietrich Braun, trans. Geoffrey W. Bromiley (New York: Seabury Press, 1981), vi.

14. Ibid., 178.

15. Ibid., 191.

16. Ibid., 194.

17. Ibid., 195.

18. Karl Barth, *Church Dogmatics* III/4, ed. and trans. G. W. Bromiley and T. F. Torrance (Edinburgh: T & T Clark, 1961), 285-86.

19. Dietrich Bonhoeffer, *Ethics*, ed. Eberhard Bethge, trans. Neville Horton Smith (New York: Macmillan, 1955), 259.

20. Ibid., 259.

21. Barth, *Church Dogmatics* III/4, 292. Barth's rejection of National Socialism is in the background of this and, for that matter, his rejection of any attempt to support the notion of a particular land being "God's country."

22. Ibid., 294.

23. Ibid., 299-302.

24. For the most recent discussion of Barth's political views see Frank Jehle, *Ever Against the Stream: The Politics of Karl Barth, 1906–1968*, trans. Richard and Martha Burnett (Grand Rapids: Eerdmans, 2002). A larger survey is available in Timothy J. Gorringe, *Karl Barth: Against Hegemony*, Christian Theology in Context (Oxford: Oxford University Press, 1999). A history of the debate over the interpretation of

Barth's politics is found in George Hunsinger, ed., *Karl Barth and Radical Politics* (Philadelphia: Westminster, 1976).

25. This is not meant to imply that Barth endured the hardships put up with by refugees in the normal sense. He was forced out of Germany but he also had a house, a job, and an official reception waiting for him when he returned to Basel from Bonn in July 1935. Charlotte von Kirschbaum, Barth's assistant, felt the move in a more dramatic fashion since she actually left behind her friends and family to continue her work with him as his assistant. See Suzanne Selinger, *Charlotte von Kirschbaum and Karl Barth: A Study in Biography and the History of Theology* (University Park, PA: Pennsylvania State University Press, 1998).

26. Karl Barth, "The Church Between East and West," in *Against the Stream: Shorter Post-War Writings*, ed. Ronald Gregor Smith (New York: Philosophical Library, 1954), 129.

27. Karl Barth, "The Christian Community in the Midst of Political Change," in Ibid., 53.

28. Ibid., 57.

29. Barth, *Church Dogmatics* III/4, 301.

30. For a description of the history of strangers in Europe see Richard J. Evans, "Social Outsiders in German History: From the Sixteenth Century to 1933," in *Social Outsiders in Nazi Germany*, ed. Robert Gellately and Nathan Stoltzfus (Princeton: Princeton University Press, 2001).

31. Guenter Lewy, *The Nazi Persecution of the Gypsies* (New York: Oxford University Press, 2000).

32. Barth himself could be uncomfortable around Jews. In a letter to Friedrich Marquardt, he admits as much, saying that he had a type of "allergic reaction" to them. See Karl Barth, *Briefe, 1961–1968*, ed. J. Fangmeier and H. Stoevesant, *Gesamtausgabe*, vol. 5 (Zurich: Theologischer Verlag, 1975), 420. Katherine Sonderegger, who cites this passage and others, considers Barth's knowledge of Judaic *thought* (emphasis added) superficial and a limiting factor in his theology, but is fervent in the position that Barth cannot be considered anti-Semitic based upon his long record of opposition to Nazi policies. See Katherine Sonderegger, *That Jesus Christ Was Born a Jew: Karl Barth's Doctrine of Israel* (University Park: Pennsylvania State University Press, 1992) and Mark R. Lindsay, *Covenanted Solidarity: The Theological Basis of Karl Barth's Opposition to Nazi Antisemitism and the Holocaust, Issues in Systematic Theology*, vol. 9 (New York: Peter Lang, 2001). It is significant that the main line of criticism of Barth's understanding of Jews *by Jews* has to do with his theology of election and not his personal relations with Jews. See the criticisms raised by Eugene B. Borowitz in "Anti-Semitism and the Christologies of Barth, Berkouwer and Pannenberg," *Dialog* 16 (winter 1977): 39.

33. Karl Barth, *Church Dogmatics* III/3, ed. and trans. G. W. Bromiley and T. F. Torrance (Edinburgh: T & T Clark, 1960), 215.

34. George Kumler Anderson, *The Legend of the Wandering Jew* (Providence: Brown University Press, 1965), 11.

35. Adolf A. Leschnitzer, "The Wandering Jew: The Alienation of the Jewish Image in Christian Consciousness," *Viator* 2 (1971): 396; Galit Hasan-Rokem and Alan Dundes, eds., *The Wandering Jew: Essays in the Interpretation of a Christian Legend* (Bloomington, IN: Indiana University Press, 1986).

36. David Welch, *Propaganda and the German Cinema 1933–1945* (London: I. B. Tauris, 2001), 248.

37. Sabine Hake, *Popular Cinema of the Third Reich* (Austin: University of Texas Press, 2001), 74.

38. Welch, *Propaganda*, 248.

39. Barth, *Church Dogmatics* III/3, 218.

40. Ibid., 219.

41. Ibid., 220.

42. Ibid., 221.

43. Ibid., 223.

44. Ibid., 224-25.

45. Karl Barth, *Church Dogmatics* III/2, ed. and trans. G. W. Bromiley and T. F. Torrance (Edinburgh: T & T Clark, 1960), 250.

46. Ibid., 251-52.

47. Ibid., 253.

48. Ibid., 263.

49. Ibid., 265.

50. John Massaro, "Press Box Propaganda? The Cold War and Sports Illustrated, 1956," *The American Journal of Popular Culture* 26, no. 3 (September 2002): 361-70.

3. "She Laid It on Us"

1. Carolyn Osiek and David L. Balch, *Families in the New Testament World: Households and House Churches* (Louisville: Westminster John Knox Press, 1997), 208.

2. In this chapter, *feminist* is taken to mean all types of theology that have in common the goal of critiquing traditions, methods, and points of view that are ignorant of or resistant to the theological concerns of women. *Feminist* means those who take liberation and empowerment to be matters of first importance. This definition includes those in North America, for example, who designate themselves as "womanist," "*mujerista*," or those who write from their own global or local perspective: Africa, Asia, Europe, South America, and so forth. There are "schools of thought" in all of these groups and they differ about the role of women's experience in theology. Serene Jones, "Women's Experience Between a Rock and a Hard Place: Feminist, Womanist, and *Mujerista* Theologies in North America," in *Horizons in Feminist Theology: Identity, Tradition, and Norms*, ed. Rebecca S. Chopp and Sheila Davaney (Minneapolis: Fortress Press, 1997), 33-53. However, I believe the limited nature of this chapter permits my generalization about who a feminist is and what a feminist does.

3. Elisabeth Schüssler Fiorenza, "Missionaries, Apostles, Co-workers: Romans 16 and the Reconstruction of Women's Early Christian History," in *Feminist Theology: A Reader*, ed. Ann Loades (Louisville: Westminster John Knox Press, 1990), 59.

4. Abraham J. Malherbe, Hamden, CT, personal correspondence, July 12, 2004.

5. Only the group in Acts 20 appears to be larger (Sopater, Aristarchus, Secundus, Gaius, Timothy, Tychichus, and Trophimus). This group, unlike Paul's companions in Acts 16, is not so much on "the mission" as they are new converts seeing Paul off as he leaves Macedonia and returns to Troas.

6. John Calvin is one of the few commentators who notices this. John Calvin, "The Acts of the Apostles 14–28," in *Calvin's Commentaries*, ed. David W. Torrance and Thomas F. Torrance, trans. John W. Fraser (Edinburgh: Oliver and Boyd, 1966), 72.

7. Stanley K. Stowers, "Letter Writing in Greco-Roman Antiquity" in *Library of Early Christianity*, ed. Wayne A. Meeks (Philadelphia: Westminster Press, 1986), 51-70.

8. Acts 15:1-3; 20:33-38; 21:1-5; Romans 15:22-24; 1 Corinthians 16:5-11; 2 Corinthians 1:14-16; Titus 3:12-13; 3 John 4–7.

9. L. Michael White, *Building God's House in the Roman World: Architectural Adaptation Among Pagans, Jews, and Christians* (Baltimore: Johns Hopkins University Press, 1990), 106.

10. Abraham J. Malherbe, *Social Aspects of Early Christianity*, 2nd ed., enlarged (Philadelphia: Fortress Press, 1983), 66.

11. Everett Ferguson, *Backgrounds of Early Christianity* (Grand Rapids: Eerdmans, 1987), 67.

12. White, *Building God's House*, 60.

13. Peter Richardson, "Early Synagogues as Collegia," in *Voluntary Associations in the Graeco-Roman World*, ed. John S. Kloppenborg and Stephen G. Wilson (London and New York: Routledge, 1996), 103.

14. L. Michael White, *The Social Origins of Christian Architecture*, vol. 2 (Valley Forge, PA: Trinity Press International, 1997), 295.

15. It is common to appeal to Josephus (*Antiquities* xiv. 10.23) and Tertullian (*Adv. Nationes*, i.13) and suggest that Jews preferred to locate synagogues near water so that they could perform their rituals. However, all that we can be sure of is that Jews in Philippi were accustomed to going to the synagogue near the river. In fact, according to Richardson, a number of Greek words are used to describe Jewish meeting places in the Diaspora: "Terminology is not crucial to the decision about what is and is not a synagogue. Buildings either for cultic or community purposes, whether *proseuchai, synodoi, sabbateia,* or *synagōgai,* all qualify." Richardson, "Early Synagogues as Collegia," 94.

16. Ivoni Richter Reimer, *Women in the Acts of the Apostles: A Feminist Libertarian Perspective*, trans. Linda M. Maloney (Minneapolis: Fortress Press, 1995), 85-90.

17. Frank Stagg, *The Book of Acts: The Early Struggle for an Unhindered Gospel* (Nashville: Broadman Press, 1955), 167.

18. Reimer, *Women*, 108.

19. Ibid., 107.

20. Ibid., 113.

21. Luise Schottroff, *Let the Oppressed Go Free: Feminist Perspectives on the New Testament* (Louisville: Westminster John Knox Press, 1993), 132.

22. Reimer, *Women*, 112.

23. Schottroff, *Let the Oppressed*, 132.

24. Plutarch, *Pericles*, 1.4, as cited in Reimer, *Women*, 107.

25. Yi-Fu Tuan, *Topophilia* (Englewood Cliffs, NJ: Prentice-Hall, 1974), 1.

26. Ibid., 93.

27. For the importance of Hurston's text in the formation of womanist ethics see Katie G. Cannon, *Black Womanist Ethics* (Atlanta: Scholars Press, 1988).

28. Zora Neale Hurston, *Their Eyes Were Watching God* (New York: HarperCollins, 1990), 191.

29. N. Lynne Westfield, *Dear Sisters: A Womanist Practice of Hospitality* (Cleveland: Pilgrim Press, 2001).

30. Ibid., 7.

31. Abraham J. Malherbe, "Conversion to Paul's Gospel," in *The Early Church in Its Context: Essays in Honor of Everett Ferguson*, ed. Abraham J. Malherbe, Fredrick W. Norris, and James W. Thompson, Supplements to *Novum Testamentum*, vol. XC (Leiden: Brill, 1998).

32. F. Scott Spenser, "Out of Mind, Out of Voice: Slave-Girls and Prophetic Daughters in Luke–Acts," *Biblical Interpretation* 7, no. 2 (1999): 147.

33. Luise Schottroff, *Lydia's Impatient Sisters: A Feminist Social History of Early Christianity*, trans. Barbara and Martin Rumscheidt (Louisville: Westminster John Knox Press, 1995), 110.

34. Letty M. Russell, *Church in the Round: Feminist Interpretation of the Church* (Louisville: Westminster John Knox Press, 1993). Russell was an early and frequent writer on hospitality and systematic theology. See Letty M. Russell, *Household of Freedom: Authority in Feminist Theology* (Philadelphia: Westminster Press, 1987); Letty M. Russell, *The Future of Partnership* (Philadelphia: Westminster Press, 1979).

35. Russell, *Church in the Round*, 21.

36. Ibid., 25.

37. Ibid., 26.

38. bell hooks, *Talking Back: Thinking Feminist, Thinking Black* (Boston: South End Press, 1989).

39. Russell, *Church in the Round*, 35.

4. "Remember My Chains"

1. http://dictionary.prisonwall.org

2. Dae Jung, Kim, *Prison Writings*, trans. Choi Sung-il and David R. McCann (Berkeley: University of California Press, 1987), 44.

3. Ibid., 204.

4. Ibid., 86.

5. Ibid., 87.

6. Ibid., 78.

7. Ibid., 53.

8. Ibid.

9. Ibid., 67.

10. Ibid., 16.

11. Ibid., 22.

12. Ibid., 19.

13. Ibid., 27.

14. Ibid., 47.

15. Ibid., 5.

16. Ibid., 9.

17. Ibid., 21.

18. Ibid., 18.

19. Ibid., 108.

20. Ibid., 5.

21. Ibid., 5-6.

22. Ibid., 107.

23. Alfred Delp S.J., *Prison Writings* (Maryknoll, NY: Orbis, 2004), 20.

24. Ibid., 15.

25. Ibid., 17.

26. Ibid., 18.

27. Ibid., 20.

28. Ibid., 17.

29. Dietrich Bonhoeffer, *Letters and Papers from Prison* (New York: Macmillan, 1972), 152.

30. Altdorfer is known to have painted at least three different *Nativity* canvases. The two most similar are the 1507 painting (Bremen, Kunsthalle) and the circa 1513 (Staatliche Museen zu Berlin). The third is different if for no other reason than the placing of the scene in an urban area (undated, Vienna, Kunsthistorisches Museum). Bonhoeffer is referring to the 1513 work.

31. Bonhoeffer, *Letters and Papers from Prison*, 152.

32. Martin Luther King, Jr., *Why We Can't Wait* (New York: Mentor, 1964), 20.

33. Taylor Branch, *Pillar of Fire: America in the King Years, 1963–65* (New York: Simon & Schuster, 1998), 114.

34. Taylor Branch, *Parting the Waters: American in the King Years, 1954–63* (New York: Simon & Schuster, 1988), 834.

35. King, *Why We Can't Wait*, 79.

36. Ibid., 80.

37. Ibid., 84.

38. Ibid., 86.

39. Ibid.

40. Ibid., 87.

41. Martin Luther King, Jr., "Notecards on Books of the Old Testament," in *Rediscovering Precious Values, July 1951–November 1955*, ed. Clayborne Carson et al., vol. II, *The Papers of Martin Luther King, Jr.* (Berkeley: University of California Press, 1994), 165.

42. The general consensus of scholars is that significant Christian sources of King's theology include the Black church tradition he grew up in, George Kelsey, Benjamin Mays, G. W. F. Hegel, Reinhold Niebuhr, Walter Rauschenbusch, L. Harold DeWolf, and Edgar Sheffield Brightman. The latter two represent "Boston Personalism," a school of thought that stressed human dignity and worth. See Ralph Burrow, Jr., "Personalism, the Objective Moral Order, and Moral Law in the Work of Martin Luther King, Jr.," in *The Legacy of Martin Luther King, Jr.: The Boundaries of Law, Politics, and Religion*, ed. Lewis Baldwin (Notre Dame, IN: University of Notre Dame Press, 2002).

43. Martin Luther King, Jr., "The Christian Pertinence of Eschatological Hope," in *Called to Serve, January 1929–June 1951*, ed. Clayborne Carson et al., vol. I, *The Papers of Martin Luther King, Jr.* (Berkeley: University of California Press, 1992), 269.

44. Ibid., 270.

45. Ibid.

46. Martin Luther King, Jr., "An Autobiography of Religious Development," in Ibid., 361-62.

47. George Hedley, *The Symbol of the Faith* (New York: Macmillian, 1948).

48. Martin Luther King, Jr., "What Experiences of Christians Living in the Early Christian Century Led to the Christian Doctrines of the Divine Sonship of Jesus, the Virgin Birth, and the Bodily Resurrection," in *Called to Serve*, 226.

49. Ibid., 272-73.

50. For this undernoticed feature of the boycott see JoAnn Gibson Robinson, *The Montgomery Bus Boycott and the Women Who Started It* (Knoxville: University of Tennessee Press, 1987).

51. Martin Luther King, Jr., "MIA Mass Meeting at Holt Street Baptist Church," in *Birth of a New Age, December 1955–December 1956*, ed. Clayborne Carson et al., vol. III, *The Papers of Martin Luther King, Jr.* (Berkeley: University of California Press, 1997), 73.

52. Ibid.

53. Ibid., 79.

54. Martin Luther King, Jr., "Testimony in State of Alabama v. M. L. King, Jr," in *Birth of a New Age*, 192.

55. Martin Luther King, Jr., "Reactions to Conviction," in Ibid., 198.

56. Keith D. Miller, *Voice of Deliverance: The Language of Martin Luther King, Jr., and Its Sources* (New York: The Free Press, 1992), 5. Putting the source of King's sermon in context gives Hamilton the credit he deserves.

57. Martin Luther King, Jr., "The Drum Major Instinct," in *A Knock at Midnight: Inspiration from the Great Sermons of Reverend Martin Luther King, Jr.*, ed. Clayborne Carson and Peter Holloran (New York: IPM/Warner Books, 1998), 185-86.

5. HOSPITALITY

1. In this section I am modifying the typology suggested by *A Stranger in the Village: Two Centuries of African-American Travel Writing*, ed. Farah J. Griffen and Cheryl J. Fish (Boston: Beacon Press, 1989).

Bibliography

Abrahams, Yvette. "Images of Sara Bartman: Sexuality, Race, and Gender in Early-Nineteenth-Century Britain." In *Nation, Empire, Colony: Historicizing Gender and Race*. Edited by Ruth Roach Pierson and Nupur Chaudhuri, 220-36. Bloomington and Indianapolis: Indiana University Press, 1998.

Anderson, George Kumler. *The Legend of the Wandering Jew*. Providence: Brown University Press, 1965.

Baldwin, Robert W. "On Earth We Are Beggars, as Christ Himself Was: The Protestant Background of Rembrandt's Imagery of Poverty, Disability, and Begging." *Konsthistorik Tidskrift* 54, no. 3 (1985): 122-35.

Barth, Karl. *Brief, 1961–1968*. Letter 260. Edited by J. Frangmeier and H. Stoevesant, 420. Vol. 5. *Gesamtausgabe*. Zurich: Theologischer Verlag, 1975.

———. "The Christian Community in the Midst of Political Change." In *Against the Stream: Shorter Post-War Writings*. Edited by Ronald Gregor Smith. New York: Philosophical Library, 1954.

———. "The Church Between East and West." In *Against the Stream: Shorter Post-War Writings*. Edited by Ronald Gregor Smith. New York: Philosophical Library, 1954.

———. *Church Dogmatics*. Edited and translated by G. W. Bromiley and T. F. Torrance. Edinburgh: T & T Clark, 1936–62.

———. *Ethics*. Edited by Dietrich Braun. Translated by Geoffrey W. Bromiley. New York: Seabury Press, 1981.

Bolchazy, Ladislaus J. *Hospitality in Early Rome: Livy's Concept of Its Humanizing Force*. Chicago: Ares Publishers, 1977.

Bonhoeffer, Dietrich. *Ethics*. Edited by Eberhard Bethge. Translated by Neville Horton Smith. New York: Macmillan Company, 1955.

———. *Letters and Papers from Prison*. New York: Macmillan, 1972.

Borowitz, Eugene B. "Anti-Semitism and the Christologies of Barth, Berkouwer and Pannenberg." *Dialog* 16 (Winter 1977): 38-41.

Burrow, Ralph, Jr. "Personalism, the Objective Moral Order, and Moral Law in the Work of Martin Luther King, Jr." In *The Legacy of Martin Luther King, Jr.: The Boundaries of Law, Politics, and Religion*. Edited by Lewis Baldwin. Notre Dame, IN: University of Notre Dame Press, 2002.

Byrne, Brendan. *The Hospitality of God: A Reading of Luke's Gospel*. Collegeville, MN: Liturgical Press, 2000.

Calvin, John. "The Acts of the Apostles 14–28." In *Calvin's Commentaries*. Edited by David W. Torrance and Thomas F. Torrance. Translated by John W. Fraser. Edinburgh: Oliver and Boyd, 1966.

Cannon, Katie G. *Black Womanist Ethics*. Atlanta: Scholars Press, 1988.

Chenu, Bruno. *The Trouble I've Seen: The Big Book of Negro Spirituals*. Translated by Eugene V. LaPlante. Valley Forge, VA: Judson Press, 2003.

Cone, James. *The Spirituals and the Blues: An Interpretation*. New York: Seabury Press, 1972.

Coulter, Ann. "This is War." National Review Online. September 13, 2001. http://www.nationalreview.com/coulter/coulter.shtml

Darden, Robert. *People Get Ready! A New History of Black Gospel Music*. New York: Continuum, 2004.

Delp, Alfred. *Prison Writings*. Maryknoll, NY: Orbis, 2004.

Derrida, Jacques. *Of Hospitality*. Translated by Rachel Bowlby. Stanford: Stanford University Press, 2000.

Dorner, I. A. *System of Christian Ethics*. Edited by A. Dorner. Translated by C. M. Mead and R. T. Cunningham. Edinburgh: T. & T. Clark, 1906.

Du Bois, W. E. B. "The Black Man in the Revolution of 1914–1918." In *Writings in Periodicals Edited by W. E. B. Du Bois: Selections from* The Crisis. Vol. 1 (1911–1925) of *The Complete Published Works of W. E. B. Du Bois*. Edited by Herbert Aptheker, 172-77. Millwood, NY: Kraus-Thomson Organization, 1983.

———. "Hopkinsville, Chicago and Idlewild." In *Writings in Periodicals Edited by W. E. B. Du Bois: Selections from* The Crisis. Vol. 1 (1911–1925) of *The Complete Published Works of W. E. B. Du Bois*. Edited by Herbert Aptheker, 305-7. Millwood, NY: Kraus-Thomson Organization, 1983.

———. "The Negro and Crime." In *Writings by W. E. B. Du Bois in Periodicals Edited by Others*. Vol. 1 (1891–1909) of *The Complete Published Works of W. E. B. Du Bois*. Edited by Herbert Aptheker, 57-59. Millwood, NY: Kraus-Thomson Organization, 1982.

———. "On Religion." In *Du Bois on Religion*. Edited by Phil Zuckerman. New York: Alta Maria, 2000.

———. *The Souls of Black Folk*. New York: Bantam Books, 1989.

———. "The Souls of White Folk." In *Darkwater: Voices from Within the Veil*, 17-29. Mineola, NY: Dover, 1999.

Epstein, Dena J. *Sinful Tunes and Spirituals: Black Folk Music to the Civil War*. Urbana, IL: University of Illinois Press, 1977.

Evans, Richard J. "Social Outsiders in German History: From the Sixteenth Century to 1933." In *Social Outsiders in Nazi Germany*. Edited by Robert Gellately and Nathan Stoltzfus. Princeton: Princeton University Press, 2001.

Ferguson, Everett. *Backgrounds of Early Christianity*. Grand Rapids: Eerdmans, 1987.

Fiorenza, Elisabeth Schüssler. "Missionaries, Apostles, Co-Workers: Romans 16 and the Reconstruction of Women's Early Christian History." In *Feminist Theology: A Reader*. Edited by Ann Loades, 57-71. Louisville: Westminster John Knox Press, 1990.

Frazier, E. Franklin. *The Negro Church*. New York: Schocken Books, 1964.

Gilmore, David, ed. *Honor and Shame and the Unity of the Mediterranean*. Washington, DC: The American Anthropological Association, 1987.

Gorringe, Timothy J. *Karl Barth: Against Hegemony*. Christian Theology in Context. Oxford: Oxford University Press, 1999.

Gregory the Great. "Epistle III, To Janurius, Bishop of Caralis." In *Nicene and Post-Nicene Fathers*. Edited by Philip Schaff and Henry Wace, 1-2. Peabody, MA: Hendrickson Publishers, 1994.

Grifffin, Farah J., and Cheryl J. Fish, eds. *A Stranger in the Village: Two Centuries of African-American Travel Writing*. Boston: Beacon Press, 1989.

Hake, Sabine. *Popular Cinema of the Third Reich*. Austin: University of Texas Press, 2001.

Harris, Michael W. *The Rise of Gospel Blues: The Music of Thomas Andrew Dorsey in the Urban Church.* New York: Oxford University Press, 1994.

Hasan-Rokem, Galit, and Alan Dundes, eds. *The Wandering Jew: Essays in the Interpretation of a Christian Legend.* Bloomington, IN: Indiana University Press, 1986.

Hedley, George. *The Symbol of the Faith.* New York: Macmillan, 1948.

Herskovits, Melville. *The Myth of the Negro Past.* Boston: Beacon Press, 1958.

hooks, bell. *Talking Back: Thinking Feminist, Thinking Black.* Boston: South End Press, 1989.

Hopkins, Dwight N. *Down, Up, and Over: Slave Religion and Black Theology.* Minneapolis: Augsburg Fortress, 2000.

Hubbard, Dolan. "Riddle Me This: Du Bois, the Sphinx, and the Crisis of Identity." In *W. E. B. Du Bois and Race: Essays Celebrating the Centennial Publication of* The Souls of Black Folk. Edited by Chester J. Fontenot Jr. and Mary Alice Morgan, 26-44. Macon, GA: Mercer University Press, 2001.

Hunsinger, George, ed. *Karl Barth and Radical Politics.* Philadelphia: Westminster, 1976.

Hurston, Zora Neale. *Their Eyes Were Watching God.* New York: HarperCollins, 1990.

Jehle, Frank. *Ever Against the Stream: The Politics of Karl Barth, 1906–1968.* Translated by Richard and Martha Burnett. Grand Rapids: Eerdmans, 2002.

John Paul II. *The Gospel of Life (Evangelium Vitae).* New York: Random House, 1995.

Jones, Arthur C. *Wade in the Water: The Wisdom of the Spirituals.* Maryknoll, NY: Orbis Books, 1993.

Jones, Serene. "Women's Experience Between a Rock and a Hard Place: Feminist, Womanist, and *Mujerista* Theologies in North America." In *Horizons in Feminist Theology: Identity, Tradition, and Norms.* Edited by Rebecca S. Chopp and Sheila Greeve Davaney, 33-53. Minneapolis: Fortress Press, 1997.

Kim, Dae Jung. *Prison Writings.* Translated by Choi Sung-il and David R. McCann. Berkeley: University of California Press, 1987.

King, Martin Luther, Jr. "An Autobiography of Religious Development." In *Called to Serve, January 1929–June 1951.* Edited by Clayborne Carson et al., 359-63. Vol. 1. *The Papers of Martin Luther King, Jr.* Berkeley: University of California Press, 1992.

———. "The Christian Pertinence of Eschatological Hope." In *Called to Serve, January 1929–June 1951.* Edited by Clayborne Carson et al., 268-73. Vol. 1. *The Papers of Martin Luther King, Jr.* Berkeley: University of California Press, 1992.

———. "The Drum Major Instinct." In *A Knock at Midnight: Inspiration from the Great Sermons of Reverend Martin Luther King, Jr.* Edited by Clayborne Carson and Peter Holloran. New York: IPM/Warner Books, 1998.

———. "MIA Mass Meeting at Holt Street Baptist Church." In *Birth of a New Age, December 1955–December 1956.* Edited by Clayborne Carson et al., 71-79.Vol. III. *The Papers of Martin Luther King, Jr.* Berkeley: University of California Press, 1997.

———. "Notecards on Books of the Old Testament." In *Rediscovering Precious Values, July 1951–November 1955.* Edited by Clayborne Carson et al., 164-67. Vol. II. *The Papers of Martin Luther King, Jr.* Berkeley: University of California Press, 1994.

———. "Reactions to Conviction." In *Birth of a New Age, December 1955–December 1956.* Edited by Clayborne Carson et al., 198-99. Vol. III. *The Papers of Martin Luther King, Jr.* Berkeley: University of California Press, 1997.

———. "Testimony in State of Alabama v. M. L. King, Jr." In *Birth of a New Age,*

December 1955–December 1956. Edited by Clayborne Carson et al., 183-97. Vol. III. *The Papers of Martin Luther King, Jr.* Berkeley: University of California Press, 1997.

———. "What Experiences of Christians Living in the Early Christian Century Led to the Christian Doctrines of the Divine Sonship of Jesus, the Virgin Birth, and the Bodily Resurrection." In *Called to Serve, January 1929–June 1951.* Edited by Clayborne Carson et al., 225-30. Vol. I. *The Papers of Martin Luther King, Jr.* Berkeley: University of California Press, 1992.

———. *Why We Can't Wait.* New York: Mentor, 1964.

Kristeva, Julia. *Strangers to Ourselves.* Translated by Leon S. Roudiez. New York: Columbia University Press, 1994.

Leschnitzer, Adolf A. "The Wandering Jew: The Alienation of the Jewish Image in Christian Consciousness." *Viator* 2 (1971): 391-96.

Levinas, Emmanuel. *Alterity and Transcendence.* New York: Columbia University Press, 1999.

Lewis, David Levering. *W. E. B. Du Bois: Biography of a Race, 1868–1919.* New York: Henry Holt, 1993.

Lewy, Guenter. *The Nazi Persecution of the Gypsies.* New York: Oxford University Press, 2000.

Lindsay, Mark R. *Covenanted Solidarity: The Theological Basis of Karl Barth's Opposition to Nazi Antisemitism and the Holocaust.* Vol. 9. *Issues in Systematic Theology.* New York: Peter Lang, 2001.

Lovell, John. *Black Song: The Forge and the Flame.* New York: Macmillan, 1972.

Luther, Martin. "Whether One May Flee from a Deadly Plague." In *Martin Luther's Basic Theological Writings.* Edited by Timothy F. Lull, 736-55. Minneapolis: Fortress Press, 1989.

Madden, Thomas F. *A Concise History of the Crusades.* Lanham, MD: Rowman & Littlefield, 1999.

Maddox, Randy L. *Responsible Grace: John Wesley's Practical Theology.* Nashville: Abingdon Press, 1994.

Malherbe, Abraham J. "Conversion to Paul's Gospel." In *The Early Church in Its Context: Essays in Honor of Everett Ferguson.* Edited by Abraham J. Malherbe, Fredrick W. Norris, and James W. Thompson. Supplements to *Novum Testamentum,* vol. XC. Leiden: Brill, 1998.

———. Hamden, CT, personal correspondence, July 12, 2004.

———. *Social Aspects of Early Christianity.* Second edition, enlarged. Philadelphia: Fortress Press, 1983.

Massaro, John. "Press Box Propaganda? The Cold War and Sports Illustrated, 1956." *The American Journal of Popular Culture* 26, no. 3 (September 2002): 361-70.

Miller, Keith D. *Voice of Deliverance: The Language of Martin Luther King, Jr. and Its Sources.* New York: The Free Press, 1992.

Mitchell, Mozella G., ed. *The Human Search: Howard Thurman and the Quest for Freedom; Proceedings of the Second Annual Thurman Convocation.* Vol. 1. Martin Luther King, Jr., Memorial Studies in Religion, Culture, and Social Development. 1. New York: Peter Lang, 1992.

Oden, Amy G. *And You Welcomed Me: A Sourcebook on Hospitality in Early Christianity.* Nashville: Abingdon Press, 2001.

Osiek, Carolyn, and David L. Balch. *Families in the New Testament World: Households and House Churches.* Louisville: Westminster John Knox Press, 1997.

Peters, Erskine. *Lyrics of the Afro-American Spiritual*. Westport, CT: Greenwood Press, 1993.

Phillips, John Edward. "The African Heritage of White America." In *Africanisms in American Culture*. Edited by Joseph Holloway. Bloomington: Indiana University Press, 1990.

Pitt-Rivers, Julian. "The Stranger, the Guest, and the Hostile Host." In *Contributions of Mediterranean Sociology*. Edited by J. G. Peristiany, 13-30. Paris: Mouton, 1968.

Pohl, Christine D. *Making Room: Recovering Hospitality as a Christian Practice*. Grand Rapids: Eerdmans, 1999.

Punshon, John. *Portrait in Grey: A Short History of the Quakers*. London: Quaker Home Service, 1984.

Raboteau, Albert J. *Slave Religion: "The Invisible Institution" in the Antebellum South*. New York: Oxford, 2004.

Reimer, Ivoni Richter. *Women in the Acts of the Apostles: A Feminist Liberation Perspective*. Translated by Linda M. Maloney. Minneapolis: Fortress Press, 1995.

Richardson, Peter. "Early Synagogues as Collegia." In *Voluntary Associations in the Graeco-Roman World*. Edited by John S. Kloppenborg and Stephen G. Wilson, 90-109. London and New York: Routledge, 1996.

Robinson, JoAnn Gibson. *The Montgomery Bus Boycott and the Women Who Started It*. Knoxville: The University of Tennessee Press, 1987.

Russell, Letty M. *Church in the Round: Feminist Interpretation of the Church*. Louisville: Westminster John Knox Press, 1993.

———. *The Future of Partnership*. Philadelphia: Westminster Press, 1979.

———. *Household of Freedom: Authority in Feminist Theology*. Philadelphia: Westminster Press, 1987.

Schottroff, Luise. *Let the Oppressed Go Free: Feminist Perspectives on the New Testament*. Louisville: Westminster John Knox Press, 1993.

———. *Lydia's Impatient Sisters: A Feminist Social History of Early Christianity*. Translated by Barbara and Martin Rumscheidt. Louisville: Westminster John Knox Press, 1995.

Selinger, Suzanne. *Charlotte von Kirschbaum and Karl Barth: A Study in Biography and the History of Theology*. University Park, PA: Pennsylvania State University Press, 1998.

Smith Jr., Luther E. *Howard Thurman: The Mystic as Prophet*. Richmond, IN: Friends United Press, 1991.

Sobel, Mechal. *Trabelin' On: The Slave Journey to an Afro-Baptist Faith*. Princeton, NJ: Princeton University Press, 1988.

Sonderegger, Katherine. *That Jesus Christ Was Born a Jew: Karl Barth's Doctrine of Israel*. University Park, PA: Pennsylvania University Press, 1992.

Spencer, F. Scott. "Out of Mind, Out of Voice: Slave-Girls and Prophetic Daughters in Luke–Acts." *Biblical Interpretation* 7, no. 2 (1999): 133-55.

Stagg, Frank. *The Book of Acts: The Early Struggle for an Unhindered Gospel*. Nashville: Broadman Press, 1955.

Stowers, Stanley K. *Letter Writing in Greco-Roman Antiquity*. In *Library of Early Christianity*. Edited by Wayne A. Meeks. Philadelphia: Westminster Press, 1986.

Tertullian. "To His Wife." In *Ante-Nicene Fathers*. Vol. IV. Edited by Phillip Schaff and James Donaldson, 39-49. New York: Hendrickson Publishers, 1994.

Thurman, Howard. *Deep River and The Negro Spiritual Speaks of Life and Death*. Richmond, IN: Friends United Press, 1975.

Trainor, Michael F. *The Quest for Home: The Household in Mark's Community.* Collegeville, MN: Liturgical Press, 2001.

Tuan, Yi-Fu. *Topophilia.* Englewood Cliffs, NJ: Prentice-Hall, 1974.

Tyerman, Christopher. *Fighting for Christendom: Holy War and the Crusades.* Oxford: Oxford University Press, 2005.

Welch, David. *Propaganda and the German Cinema 1933–1945.* London: I. B. Tauris, 2001.

Westfield, N. Lynne. *Dear Sisters: A Womanist Practice of Hospitality.* Cleveland: Pilgrim Press, 2001.

White, L. Michael. *Building God's House in the Roman World: Architectural Adaptation Among Pagans, Jews, and Christians.* Baltimore: Johns Hopkins University Press, 1990.

———. *The Social Origins of Christian Architecture.* Valley Forge, PA: Trinity Press International, 1997.

Williams, Delores S. *Sisters in the Wilderness: The Challenge of Womanist God-Talk.* Maryknoll, NY: Orbis, 1993.

Work, John Wesley. *Folk Song of the American Negro.* Westport, CT: Greenwood Press, 1969.

Zeid, A. M. Abou. "Honour and Shame Among the Bedouin of Egypt." In *Honour and Shame: The Values of Mediterranean Society.* Edited by J. G. Peristiany, 245-59. London: Weidenfeld and Nicolson, 1965.